OVERVIEW

Overview

Preparing for difficult conversations is an important part of effective communication in the workplace. A difficult conversation is one where emotions are involved, there's an element of risk, and the exchange has the potential for confrontation.

When you're preparing for a difficult conversation, don't avoid the situation. Make sure your goal for the conversation is clear, realistic, and relevant. And make sure to choose an appropriate time and place to have the conversation.

There are four steps to changing a negative internal monologue to a positive internal monologue. Step one is to be aware of your negative inner voice. Step two is to consider both positive and negative possible outcomes of having the conversation. Step three is to focus on the goal of the conversation. And step four is to develop a positive internal monologue by reframing negative thoughts in a positive way.

Preparing for a difficult conversation involves analyzing the practical and emotional levels of the conversation, and then planning your approach.

Guidelines for analyzing the practical level are to consider the other person's perspective, consider your own viewpoint, make sure you understand the situation, make sure you don't assign blame, admit your mistakes, and reverse roles to consider the other side of things.

Analyzing the emotional level involves managing both your emotions and the other person's emotions. Planning the conversation involves identifying your goal, outlining the structure of the conversation, and rehearsing the conversation.

When you're preparing for a difficult conversation, it's imperative to examine your own attitude toward the conversation. Your mind-set is the logical thinking that determines how you interpret and respond to communication. The right mind-set will make it easier to communicate effectively and reach the goal of your conversation. The four qualities of an appropriate mind-set are being open-minded, collaborative, empathic, and engaged.

Having a difficult conversation, and making it progress well, requires following a clear structure. It should also involve adopting an appropriate communication style to suit the individual and the context.

There are five steps to creating progress in a difficult conversation. First, open with an agenda. Second, invite dialogue. Third, share views and perspectives to learn from each other. Fourth, look for a mutual understanding, and finally, design an action plan.

Managing Difficult Conversations

Your communication style throughout the conversation is crucial to a positive outcome. It's important that you're clear and direct, and focus on the facts. You need to be honest and fair to your colleague. Also, be assertive but tactful, and listen effectively.

Once a difficult conversation is opened well, the second step is inviting dialogue. This involves connecting with the other person by using strength-focused communication.

Strength-focused communication can keep others engaged. This involves speaking to a person's strengths, acknowledging feelings, and understanding the benefits of another approach.

The third step – sharing views – should follow the guidelines of prioritizing, focusing on facts, being flexible, and sharing relevant information. Reaching a mutual understanding is the fourth step, and can be achieved by asking for views, empathizing, and reframing.

Finally, you can then design an action plan with your colleague.

You've now had the opportunity to practice having a difficult conversation with an employee. To reach a successful outcome, it's always important to open a difficult conversation with an agenda. Then you can use strength-focused communication to invite meaningful dialogue.

When sharing your views and perspectives, discuss what's important first, and present the situation with a focus on facts. It's important to share all relevant information while maintaining an open mind about your views.

Ask your colleague for views and perspectives, and respond by empathizing and reframing the facts. You should then be in a position to come to a mutual understanding of the situation. You can then create an action plan together.

The appropriate communication style for any dialogue is to keep the focus on facts. Being clear and direct can help you achieve this. Be honest and fair to your colleague, while also being assertive but tactful. It's also important to listen carefully to learn from the conversation.

There are several challenges that you may encounter in a difficult work-related conversation. These challenges can include situations in which the other person doesn't engage in the dialogue, the conversation takes a destructive direction, or you become challenged by your own emotions.

To deal with a person who doesn't engage, you can comment on the person's reaction and take control by asking questions. If a conversation takes a destructive direction, you reframe unhelpful statements. And if you become challenged by your own emotions during a conversation, you can create validation and manage your response to criticism.

There are many benefits of being able to reframe a conversation. You can keep the conversation on track, you can influence the person's perspective, you can increase a person's willingness to engage, and you can achieve a mutually acceptable solution.

To reframe a conversation, listen carefully to the other person and extract the core ideas. Then use these ideas to develop relevant concepts that are more constructive and will help get the conversation back on track. Finally, you need to persist using this technique to keep the conversation on track.

Sometimes, during a difficult conversation, your emotions may get the better of you. One of the most common triggers that can cause you to lose control of your emotions is when you sense that the other person's behavior is wrong. You create validation by normalizing the other person's feelings. This helps you to suppress your fight or flight reactions. Validation can be carried out at three levels: acknowledgment, acceptance, and identification.

When you're criticized during a difficult conversation you may experience strong emotions. This can also lead you to experiencing fight or flight reactions, which can jeopardize the outcome of the conversation.

There are steps that you can follow to handle criticism in a difficult conversation. The first step is to recognize your own reactions. The second step is to listen. The third step is to ask questions using a neutral tone. And the final step is to respond by either agreeing, disagreeing, or asking for more time.

PREPARING FOR A DIFFICULT CONVERSATION

Preparing for a Difficult Conversation

As a manager, communication is arguably the most important skill you can possess. It's the ability managers use most – to motivate, inspire, and celebrate achievement with employees, colleagues, and superiors. But sometimes managers need to use communication skills to have difficult conversations – to communicate bad news or unpopular decisions, or to reveal something uncomfortable, awkward, embarrassing, or even hurtful.

So what exactly is a difficult conversation? Difficult conversations share three characteristics that separate them from other communication. In a difficult conversation, emotions are involved, there's an element of risk, and the exchange has the potential for confrontation.

When you're exposed to a difficult situation that needs to be discussed, you shouldn't avoid the conversation. A tendency to avoid difficult conversations can reduce your credibility as an effective manager. You should only have conversations that have a realistic and relevant goal. Once you've determined the need to have the conversation, then you should make sure to choose an appropriate time and place.

Even when conversations are particularly risky or challenging, you shouldn't avoid having them. Unresolved and mishandled issues can escalate into much more serious problems. These can sometimes cause permanent damage to productivity and to personal relationships.

Stressful events such as preparing for a difficult conversation can often result in a negative internal monologue. To deal effectively with difficult conversations, you'll need to recognize your negative internal monologue and replace it with one that's positive.

There are four steps to changing your negative internal monologue into a positive one. Step one is to be aware of your negative inner voice. Step two is to consider both positive and negative possible outcomes of having the conversation. Step three is to focus on the goal of the conversation. And step four is to develop a positive internal monologue to deal with the stress and anxiety of having the conversation.

Good preparation involves being aware of five common mistakes managers make when they're involved in difficult conversations. The five mistakes are making assumptions about the other person's behavior, being adamant about your own viewpoint, blaming the other person, disregarding emotion, and not acknowledging the personal impact on your own identity.

You can prepare for a difficult conversation in four stages. You need to analyze the practical level, as well as the emotional level. Then identify the goal of the conversation, and plan the conversation.

Your first stage is to analyze the practical level of the conversation. An important part of this practical analysis is to consider the other person's perspective. You should be open and willing to listen to the other person's views.

Your second stage in preparing for a difficult conversation is to analyze the emotional level of the conversation. Feeling emotional can make you uncomfortable and vulnerable. Likewise, it's difficult to know how to respond when other people display emotion. But it's only at the emotional level that many aspects of a difficult conversation can be addressed. Preparation for a difficult conversation involves both managing your emotions and managing the other person's emotions.

The third stage in preparing for a difficult conversation is to identify your goal. If you define your goal in advance, you can stay focused on the reason for the conversation. This means you need to clearly identify what you want to accomplish.

The fourth stage in preparing for a difficult conversation is to plan the conversation. Difficult conversations can be stressful and even unpleasant. This means some managers avoid having difficult conversations until forced to deal with the matter, and then go into the situation ill-prepared. Before you have a conversation, it's important to outline the structure of the conversation, and rehearse your approach to achieving your goal.

Mediating disputes, delivering bad news, talking about performance, and counseling employees are all part of being an effective leader. But these difficult conversations can be risky for managers who don't have the right mind-set. It's important to prepare what you're going to communicate by analyzing the practical and emotional levels, setting a clear goal, and planning a strategic path. But it's just as important to prepare how you're going to communicate by examining your own attitude toward the conversation.

You can't predict exactly how a difficult conversation will unfold. But an appropriate mind-set can help you choose the appropriate words, tone, and responses to steer the discussion in the right direction. Your conversation should reflect each of the four qualities of an appropriate mind-set – being open-minded, collaborative, empathic, and engaged.

HAVING A DIFFICULT CONVERSATION

Having a difficult conversation

As a manager, communication is arguably the most important skill you can possess. It's the ability managers use most – to motivate, inspire, and celebrate achievement with employees, colleagues, and superiors. But sometimes managers need to use communication skills to have difficult conversations – to communicate bad news or unpopular decisions, or to reveal something uncomfortable, awkward, embarrassing, or even hurtful.

Consider Mario, a manager at an insurance company. Lee is a junior manager at the company and Mario has worked with her on several projects. Recently, Mario led a team that interviewed Lee for a project management position. Follow along as Mario has a difficult conversation with Lee.

Lee: Hi! Do you have a minute?
Lee is pleasant.
Mario: Um...hi, Lee. Sure. Sit down. Listen, I've been meaning to talk to you.

Lee: So, what's going on with the project manager job? I haven't heard anything.
Lee is persistent.
Mario: Look, Lee....I meant to meet with you before this, but I've been busy.
Mario is overly cheerful.
Lee: OK. So what's up?
Lee is suspicious.
Mario: I'm sorry, but the team gave the position to Janet last week.
Mario is sincere.
Lee: Last week? Oh no. I work with Janet. This morning I was saying I hoped I'd get this job. What if she overheard me? This is so humiliating!
Lee is upset.
Mario: Look, you're a real good manager. But Janet was just a better fit for this particular position. Other opportunities will come your way.
Mario is reassuring.
Lee: Well, if they do, I hope someone will get around to telling me before I make a fool of myself again.
Lee is annoyed.

It's clear that Mario could have been more effective in his approach to holding a difficult conversation. He initially avoided the conversation, until Lee confronted him. This procrastination contributed to her distress. Although he was engaged in the conversation and empathic to Lee, Mario may have permanently damaged his working relationship with her. He would have definitely benefited from being better prepared for this conversation.

BENEFITS OF BEING PREPARED

Benefits of being prepared

So what exactly is a difficult conversation? Difficult conversations share three characteristics that separate them from other communication. In a difficult conversation, emotions are involved, there's an element of risk, and the exchange has the potential for confrontation.

See each characteristic of a difficult conversation for more information.

Emotions involved

Difficult conversations involve many different types of emotions. You may feel fear or embarrassment at having to bring up something sensitive. The person you're talking to might feel shock, resentment, or anger at the subject of the conversation.

Element of risk

Difficult conversations always involve an element of risk, and the consequences or stakes can be significant. It's important to proceed cautiously. A rejected or misinterpreted conversation has the potential to permanently damage a relationship. If not presented well, a query could be perceived as an accusation, or a request misinterpreted as a threat.

Potential for confrontation

Difficult conversations are a challenge because what you have to say may not be well received. Recipients may feel under attack, reject your message outright, or mistake your candor for tactlessness. Both parties may get swept up in strong emotion and lose control.

Question

Management roles often involve situations that require having difficult conversations.

What do you think are examples of a difficult conversation?

Options:

1. You have to lay off a long-time employee
2. You need to request that your client give you an extension to finish a project
3. You have to tell a colleague that his rude behavior is unacceptable to you
4. You have to meet with your office manager to review travel arrangements for a business trip
5. You need to notify your boss that your latest assignment is on schedule

Answer:

Option 1: This option is correct. Difficult conversations are those that involve emotions. This conversation could be traumatic for the employee and stressful for you.

Option 2: This option is correct. Difficult conversations involve an element of risk. Mishandling this conversation could permanently damage your relationship with your client.

Option 3: This option is correct. Difficult conversations have the potential for confrontation. Your colleague may not agree with your assessment of his behavior.

Option 4: This option is incorrect. This routine conversation is unlikely to be emotional, risky, or confrontational.

Option 5: This option is incorrect. This is a normal part of doing business. Just notifying your boss that everything is fine may not even require a face-to-face conversation. An e-mail or memo may do just as well.

Being prepared for a difficult conversation gives you time to think things over and clarify your own position on the issue.

It allows you time to reflect on how the conversation might impact your relationships with the other person involved. It also helps you overcome your own fear of dealing with sensitive or emotional issues.

It's important that you take responsibility for having a difficult conversation when it's needed and that you take the steps necessary to help you manage the conversation effectively. Addressing issues in a timely and positive manner through effective conversations will help improve performance within your work unit and reinforce your leadership.

Question

How might you benefit from being prepared for a difficult conversation?

Options:

1. You're less likely to avoid a conversation when you're prepared for it

2. You'll be better able to deal with your emotions about having the conversation

3. It will help improve performance within your work unit

4. You'll be perceived as a more accountable manager

5. You'll be well liked by clients, employees, and colleagues

6. You'll be able to have fewer difficult conversations in the future

Answer:

Option 1: This option is correct. Being prepared helps you realize there's no perfect time and place for a difficult conversation. It also helps you deal with your fear of doing or saying the wrong thing.

Option 2: This option is correct. Preparing for a difficult conversation can help you face emotions such as fear and apprehension.

Option 3: This option is correct. Being prepared for a conversation will help you communicate more effectively about issues within your work unit, and will contribute to improved performance.

Option 4: This option is correct. Taking responsibility for having difficult conversations will enhance the perception of your personal accountability.

Option 5: This option is incorrect. Being prepared for a conversation does help you resolve issues more effectively, but its purpose isn't to make people like you.

Option 6: This option is incorrect. Having difficult conversations is part of being a manager. However, preparation will help you ensure your conversations are more efficient and effective.

WHEN TO HAVE A DIFFICULT CONVERSATION

When to have a difficult conversation

When you're exposed to a difficult situation that needs to be discussed, you shouldn't avoid the conversation. A tendency to avoid difficult conversations can reduce your credibility as an effective manager. You should only have conversations that have a realistic and relevant goal. Once you've determined the need to have the conversation, then you should make sure to choose an appropriate time and place.

Even when conversations are particularly risky or challenging, you shouldn't avoid having them. Unresolved and mishandled issues can escalate into much more serious problems. These can sometimes cause permanent damage to productivity and to personal relationships.

Anthony is a manager who has trouble having difficult conversations. Sensitive or emotional issues make him uncomfortable.

He worries about not being liked and respected or about being perceived as a nag. He feels pressured to do

Managing Difficult Conversations

the right thing but fears the emotional fallout of facing that responsibility.

Anthony avoids difficult conversations by "waiting until the time is right." But the perfect set of circumstances he's waiting for rarely occurs. And the longer he waits, the more difficult it becomes to address issues. So instead of being respected, Anthony is perceived as a manager who isn't accountable for his own work.

You may have noted that when you can't think of a productive outcome, it may actually be detrimental to have a difficult conversation.

Also, it's just not practical or effective to discuss every decision, issue, or infraction you encounter at work. That's why it's important to "pick your battles" when deciding whether or not to talk about something.

You should also consider that not every issue at work will be your responsibility to deal with. If you overdo it, you'll run the risk of alienating others or being branded as a "busybody" or a "whiner." And people may just stop listening to you completely.

When you're deciding whether to have a conversation, make sure you have a realistic and relevant goal. Ask yourself if anything really productive can come out of discussing an issue.

Will a discussion change the situation or behavior that's causing issues? Is there a better solution or a more effective method of communication?

It can help to practice phrasing your goal as a specific and reasonable request – for example "Would you be willing to alter this process?"

Now imagine you've decided to have a difficult conversation with an employee and you're clear about the goal of the conversation. Do you think it would be appropriate to initiate the difficult conversation in the elevator as you're on the way home from work? What about bringing up an issue six months after it happened? If you answered "no," you're aware that good preparation includes choosing an appropriate time and place for a difficult conversation.

When you're planning for a difficult conversation, the right timing can make a big difference. Make sure to wait to have the conversation until you're calm and collected, but don't wait so long that the issue becomes "stale" or intensifies.

Plan the conversation for a time of day that's convenient for both of you, and give the other person time to prepare before the meeting.

Atmosphere is also important. Choose a comfortable, private setting without distractions and where neither of you will be interrupted.

Make sure to schedule enough time to fully engage in the conversation. Make sure the other person has time to speak. Keep in mind that the person you're talking to may want to ask questions or raise objections to what you have to say. Try to anticipate these concerns and plan to give yourself enough time to respond confidently.

Question

Before having a difficult conversation with someone, what are guidelines you should follow?

Options:

1. Don't avoid difficult conversations

2. Have a discussion goal that's clear, realistic, and relevant

3. Make sure it's the right time and place

4. Ensure the discussion won't interfere with your workday

5. Take the opportunity to have the conversation the next time you run into the person

Answer:

Option 1: This option is correct. Even when conversations are particularly risky or challenging, you shouldn't avoid having them.

Option 2: This option is correct. A serious discussion isn't necessary for every issue that comes up at work. Make sure you have a clear and appropriate goal before you initiate a difficult conversation.

Option 3: This option is correct. It's important to have the discussion at a time and place that will facilitate an effective outcome for the conversation.

Option 4: This option is incorrect. A difficult discussion will involve more than one person. You should have the discussion at a time and place that is comfortable and appropriate for both parties.

Option 5: This option is incorrect. It's not effective to bring up an issue for discussion without preparation, or when the other party isn't expecting it.

THE INTERNAL MONOLOGUE

The internal monologue

Have you ever silently given yourself a pep talk, or practiced an upcoming conversation in your mind? The little voice in your mind that's continually weighing options and assessing how well you're performing is known as your "internal monologue." Whether or not you're aware of it, your internal monologue is going on almost all the time – dredging up old experiences, comparing you to your coworkers, and either pushing you into a situation or advising you to avoid it.

Stressful events such as preparing for a difficult conversation can often result in a negative internal monologue.

To deal effectively with difficult conversations, you'll need to recognize your negative internal monologue and replace it with one that's positive.

DEALING WITH YOUR INTERNAL MONOLOGUE

Dealing with your internal monologue

Carmen is a senior sales manager working for a large communications company. This morning, Carmen left for work in a positive frame of mind. And why not? After all, she'd met her monthly sales targets and her boss was pleased with the results. But upon arriving at the office, Carmen begins to feel anxious. Today she's meeting with Ross, a salesperson, to tell him he won't be getting a bonus this quarter.

As the morning progresses, thoughts begin to race through Carmen's mind. Ross hadn't met his sales targets, but what if he reacts badly anyway? He's popular with the other employees. What if she loses the respect of the whole department? Carmen is feeling really negative now, almost in a panic. What if everyone thinks she's taken her own bonus at Ross's expense? She begins to think she'd be better off sending him an e-mail to communicate the news.

Carmen is in her office when her colleague James pops by. Follow along as Carmen and James discuss her impending conversation with Ross.

James: What's up? You look a little stressed. Got some deadline looming?

James is friendly.

Carmen: No. It's just...well, I'm supposed to talk to one of my salespeople this afternoon about quarterly bonuses. He didn't make his targets, so no bonus for him.

Carmen is reluctant.

James: Whoa! He won't be very pleased to hear that.

James is apprehensive.

Carmen: Don't I know it. But you make your targets or you don't. He's just so emotional. What if he loses his temper, or threatens to quit? Oh man, what if he starts crying? I can't deal with that.

Carmen is anxious.

James: Those conversations are never any fun. Can you avoid it somehow?

James is sympathetic.

Carmen: I could send him an e-mail...no, that's not professional. He deserves to be told in person. And besides I want to motivate him. Remind him he's got another shot at those targets next quarter.

Carmen explains.

James: Good enough reason to talk to him then.

James is convincing.

Carmen: Yeah. If only I could get rid of that little voice in my head telling me it's going to be a disaster.

Carmen sighs.

Carmen is clearly stressed about the conversation she has to have with Ross. The little voice – her internal monologue – is relaying negative messages about what might happen.

Although she could avoid the conversation, Carmen realizes that it wouldn't be very professional. She knows that, in the long run, the most effective way to manage the situation is to talk to Ross in person.

To effectively prepare for her conversation, Carmen will need to change her negative internal monologue to a positive one.

Question

How do you rate your own internal monologue?

Options:

1. Mainly negative
2. Sometimes negative, sometimes positive
3. Mainly positive

Answer:

Option 1: You indicated that your internal monologue is mainly negative. Negative thoughts are very stressful. To prepare for a conversation, you'll need to replace your negative internal monologue with a positive and self-affirming alternative.

Option 2: You indicated that your internal monologue is sometimes negative and sometimes positive. It's natural for mood and emotion to affect your internal monologue. Learning to manage your thoughts will help you tip the balance back to a positive internal monologue when you need to.

Option 3: You indicated that your internal monologue is mainly positive. This is a good foundation for preparing for difficult conversations. But anyone can start to have negative thoughts when stress levels rise. It's always helpful to learn how to recognize and cope with a negative internal monologue.

MANAGING A NEGATIVE INTERNAL MONOLOGUE

Managing a negative internal monologue

There are four steps to changing your negative internal monologue into a positive one. Step one is to be aware of your negative inner voice. Step two is to consider both positive and negative possible outcomes of having the conversation. Step three is to focus on the goal of the conversation. And step four is to develop a positive internal monologue to deal with the stress and anxiety of having the conversation.

The first step in changing your negative internal monologue is to be aware of your negative inner voice.

Your inner voice serves an important purpose. It's what allows you to use your judgment and objectively weigh your options before deciding on how to proceed.

But your inner voice can also consist of negative thoughts that challenge your judgment and self-esteem. It warns you about the worst that can happen, saying you'll fail, you'll embarrass yourself, people won't like you, or you'll make them mad. If you let it, a negative inner voice can grow stronger, promoting fear and anxiety, and painting a negative picture of your abilities as a manager. But once you're aware of your inner voice, you'll be able to challenge it.

The second step in changing your negative internal monologue is to consider the possible outcomes of having the conversation.

Consider all the potential outcomes of having the conversation – not just the negative ones. Take time in advance to imagine the conversation, considering the implications of how you might react in different situations.

Of course you can't always predict another person's reaction to what you have to say. But you'll be more confident when you're prepared to be agile in your approach to what you're trying to communicate and how you deliver your message.

Consider Mel. He's preparing to have a difficult conversation with his colleague Andrew. Mel has been letting Andrew share his small office, but it's not working out. Mel is preparing to tell Andrew to leave, but he's worrying about all the things that could go wrong. Mel realizes he has to change his negative internal monologue to a positive one. His first two steps will be to become aware of his negative inner voice and to consider both positive and negative possible outcomes.

See each of the first two steps for an example of how Mel begins to change his negative internal monologue to a positive one.

Be aware of negative inner voice

The first thing Mel does is become aware of his negative inner voice. He listens for the negative messages that challenge his decision to confront Andrew. He realizes his negative voice is telling him that he's being selfish and that Andrew won't like him anymore.

Consider possible outcomes

In step two, Mel considers both positive and negative possible outcomes of having the conversation with Andrew. He worries Andrew might be hurt or angry. But Mel also considers that sharing the cramped office is having a detrimental effect on both his and Andrew's productivity. He realizes that not dealing with the issue could permanently damage his working relationship with Andrew. Mel's confidence begins to grow as he prepares how he might respond to each possibility.

The third step in changing your negative internal monologue is to focus on the goal of the conversation. When you're preparing for a difficult conversation, you should think of your goal as your destination point.

There are a number of reasons for focusing on your goal. You may have noted that a clear goal defines the purpose of the conversation and makes the encounter less threatening.

It can also frame the discussion by giving it a beginning and an end point. This helps to deal with anxiety and fear of the unknown.

You also may have noted that focusing on your goal will prepare you to engage the other person in envisioning a positive outcome for the meeting.

The fourth step in changing your negative internal monologue is to develop a positive internal monologue. This involves "reframing" – taking your negative thoughts and translating them into something helpful.

If preparing for a conversation triggers a negative internal monologue, stop and think about whether there's a positive reason behind that train of thought. What is it your inner voice is trying to achieve?

Perhaps you're trying to protect yourself from failure. Reframing allows you to consider positive ways to achieve the same intention. Instead of "I can't afford to fail," change your perspective to "Here's what I can achieve."

It can also help to turn the negative thought into a question. For example, "He'll hate me if I tell him" might become "How can I minimize the impact of this conversation on our relationship?" Or "This will never work" becomes "How can I make this work?"

Remember Mel? He's still working on managing his negative internal monologue so he can have a conversation with his coworker, Andrew.

Mel's third step is to focus on the goal of his conversation – to move Andrew out of the office. This goal gives him a starting point and ending point for the conversation.

Mel's final step is to develop a positive internal monologue. He takes his negative thoughts and reframes them positively. So "I'm a mean person to kick Andrew out" gets reframed as "I'll be a more efficient manager when I can work in peace."

Question

Kendra is preparing to have a talk with her boss, but she's worried it won't go well.

What are examples of steps to change Kendra's negative internal monologue to a positive one?

Options:

1. She tries to be conscious of thoughts that are impeding her ability to use her judgment in a productive way

Managing Difficult Conversations

2. She envisions the different ways the conversation might progress, and how she would deal with each situation

3. She makes sure she's clear about the purpose of the conversation

4. She reframes her thoughts so they have a positive intent

5. She focuses only on the positive possible outcomes of having the conversation

6. She ignores her negative thoughts so they won't cause fear and anxiety

Answer:

Option 1: This option is correct. The first step in changing a negative internal monologue is to be aware of the negative inner voice.

Option 2: This option is correct. The second step in changing a negative internal monologue is to consider possible outcomes of having the conversation.

Option 3: This option is correct. The third step in changing a negative internal monologue is to focus on the goal of the conversation.

Option 4: This option is correct. The fourth step in changing a negative internal monologue is to develop a positive internal monologue. Reframing can help turn negative thoughts into positive intent.

Option 5: This option is incorrect. She'll be better prepared if she considers both positive and negative possible outcomes of having a difficult conversation.

Option 6: This option is incorrect. Negative thoughts may have a reason behind them. Better to cope with emotions by reframing negative thoughts in a positive way.

COMMON MISTAKES

Common mistakes

Talking to people can resolve many different workplace issues. But sometimes when people talk, things get worse. Emotions escalate, misunderstandings ensue, and relationships suffer.

Good preparation involves being aware of five common mistakes managers make when they're involved in difficult conversations. The five mistakes are making assumptions about the other person's behavior, being adamant about your own viewpoint, blaming the other person, disregarding emotion, and not acknowledging the personal impact on your own identity.

See each mistake for more information.

Making assumptions about the other person's behavior

One of the biggest mistakes you can make is to assume you understand the intent behind the other person's behavior. This often involves confusing the impact of the issue with the intention of the other person. So "I felt angry" becomes "She did that to make me angry." This in turn spills over into the conversation as an accusation, generating resistance and defensiveness.

Being adamant about your own viewpoint

It's important to focus on your goal, but being adamant that you're right is not an attitude that will help the conversation progress. You need to be open to the other person's views.

Blaming the other person

Playing the "blame game" is counterproductive. Rather than encouraging people to accept responsibility, accusations provoke them to push back, turning the conversation into an argument.

Disregarding emotion

Difficult conversations aren't just about facts. They also involve emotion. Some managers think they have to ignore emotions in order to stay rational about the issue under discussion. But feelings are an integral part of difficult conversations. It's vital to acknowledge emotions before you can develop an empathic understanding of the other person.

Not acknowledging personal impact

Difficult conversations involve facing other people, but they can also involve facing how you view yourself. Some managers make the mistake of not acknowledging and preparing for this impact. For example, a defensive or accusatory reaction from someone can impact a manager's confidence and self-worth.

You can avoid many common mistakes through careful preparation for your conversation. Before you go into the conversation, you should be clear about your rationale for the discussion.

And be sure you understand your desired results from having the conversation – the goals and objectives you want to achieve by having the conversation.

Preparation can also help you develop emotional resilience. When you examine your feelings before a conversation, it helps you consider the emotional impact it could have on your identity.

ANALYZING THE PRACTICAL LEVEL

Analyzing the practical level

You can prepare for a difficult conversation in four stages. You need to analyze the practical level, as well as the emotional level. Then identify the goal of the conversation, and plan the conversation.

Your first stage is to analyze the practical level of the conversation. An important part of this practical analysis is to consider the other person's perspective. You should be open and willing to listen to the other person's views.

You should also consider your own viewpoint. Are you making any assumptions or judgments that don't have a basis in fact? It's important to shift away from these presuppositions and focus on facts.

It's also important to make sure you really understand the situation. Think about the other person's frame of reference. For example, are there any influences or motivations you're not aware of? It can be valuable to talk to other people who know the person, or who were involved in the issue.

Blame often plays a part in serious work issues. Who made the mistake? Who didn't follow the rules? Who neglected responsibility? But focusing a conversation on blame produces disagreement and denial. Don't assign blame. Instead, move toward exploring solutions.

Not all difficult conversations are about someone else's mistakes. It's one thing to step back and consider how someone else contributed to a problem, but it's quite another to be objective about your own contribution. When it's relevant, admit your own mistakes. Determine why those mistakes happened, and explain how you intend to mitigate the situation.

Reversing roles is a technique that can help you prepare for the other person's responses to the conversation. Think to yourself, "If our roles were reversed, what would I say, how would I react, and how would I feel?"

Consider Rajat, a senior manager at Sonical Software. He's just received a security report that Katherine, one of his direct reports, was seen carrying a company laptop off the premises. The chief of security is concerned she might be stealing. Katherine has not been assigned a personal laptop, and removing company property from the building is not allowed. Rajat decides he needs to have a conversation with Katherine.

See each guideline for analyzing the practical level of a difficult conversation for an example of how Rajat prepared for his conversation with Katherine.

Consider the other person's perspective

Rajat asks himself why Katherine would have removed the laptop. He considers Katherine's viewpoint and acknowledges that perhaps she needed it for work and didn't understand the rules.

Consider your own viewpoint

A few years ago, Rajat had a problem with staff theft within his team and he had to take disciplinary measures. Rajat realizes that he can't let this incident influence his own viewpoint. He needs to be objective and unbiased about the situation.

Understand the situation

Rajat makes sure he has all the facts by talking to the chief of security. He finds out that Katherine carried the laptop out in full sight of security, without trying to hide it.

Don't assign blame

Rajat notes the facts of the case. He's annoyed about Katherine's actions, but doesn't focus on blame. He decides to present the issue to her in terms of the facts – that she removed a laptop from the premises.

Admit your mistakes

Rajat considers whether he has any responsibility for the incident. He has to admit that although he trained Katherine, he doesn't remember mentioning company policy about removing equipment.

Reverse roles

Rajat tries to gain insight into the issue by reversing roles. If he were Katherine, he might argue that it was OK just this once, or that he needed the laptop to meet a deadline. He prepares an answer for each argument he envisions Katherine might make.

Consider this example. Mai and her direct report Lincoln work for a large property development company. Lincoln has been part of the succession planning program for three years. A management position has recently become vacant and Lincoln has decided to apply. He's provided Mai's name as a reference without first asking her. Mai doesn't think Lincoln's ready for management yet, and she determines she'll need to prepare to discuss the issue with him.

Question

What are examples of Mai following the guidelines for analyzing the practical level of preparing a difficult conversation?

Options:

1. Mai considers whether she may have inadvertently encouraged Lincoln to apply for a promotion by praising his work

2. Mai talks to her assistant, and discovers Lincoln had left a voicemail asking for a reference, but no one had called him back

3. Mai admits that she sometimes ignores Lincoln's phone calls

4. Mai imagines the conversation and considers how she would react if she were Lincoln

5. Mai notes a number of reasons why Lincoln is doing the wrong thing by using her name as a reference

6. Mai plans to tell Lincoln that she'll never write a good reference for him because of his behavior

Answer:

Option 1: This option is correct. It's important to consider the other person's perspective when you're planning to talk to him.

Option 2: This option is correct. By talking to her colleagues, Mai discovered a fact that might help her understand the situation.

Option 3: This option is correct. Admitting your mistakes is an important part of preparing for a conversation.

Option 4: This option is correct. Reversing roles can help you prepare for the other person's reactions during the conversation.

Option 5: This option is incorrect. Assigning blame isn't productive. Mai should look for the real cause of the issue.

Option 6: This option is incorrect. Mai should consider Lincoln's perspective. He may not think there's anything wrong with his behavior. She's better off to work on a positive solution to the issue.

ANALYZING THE EMOTIONAL LEVEL

Analyzing the emotional level

Your second stage in preparing for a difficult conversation is to analyze the emotional level of the conversation. Feeling emotional can make you uncomfortable and vulnerable. Likewise, it's difficult to know how to respond when other people display emotion. But it's only at the emotional level that many aspects of a difficult conversation can be addressed. Preparation for a difficult conversation involves both managing your emotions and managing the other person's emotions.

The first step toward managing your emotions involves acknowledging that you have them. This isn't as simple as it sounds.

Many managers equate being professional with staying completely calm and rational. They believe that emotion clouds their judgment and makes them weak.

For other managers, the problem isn't that they don't express feelings, but that they can't control them. Instead of acknowledging emotions, they get angry and lose their temper. They lash out with accusations that are embarrassing or hurtful to the other person.

Acknowledging your emotions will help you deal with them in a constructive way. Start by naming them and asking yourself "Are my feelings valid or appropriate?" It's often difficult to decide how much emotion to share. Try to find the middle ground between reticence and complete disclosure. This is where you'll start your conversation. Then, during the conversation you'll be prepared to either step back or share more of your emotions if you need to.

Remember Rajat and Katherine? Rajat is preparing to talk to Katherine about the fact she was seen removing a company laptop from the workplace. Now that Rajat has analyzed the practical level of the conversation, he needs to analyze the emotional level. The first stage is acknowledging his own emotional reaction to the situation. This involves acknowledging his own emotions, and finding the emotional middle ground.

See each guideline for analyzing the emotional level of a difficult conversation for an example of how Rajat prepared for his conversation with Katherine.

Acknowledge emotions

Rajat names the emotions he's feeling about having to have the conversation. He notes that he's angry that Katherine precipitated the issue. He's embarrassed that Security reported one of his staff members. He's disappointed that Katherine didn't follow the rules, and he's scared she may actually have stolen the laptop.

Find the middle ground

Rajat examines his emotions to find the middle ground. He decides to tell Katherine that he's disappointed she broke the rules, and embarrassed that Security came to him about the issue. But he decides to hold back revealing his other emotions until he hears Katherine's side of the story.

The second part of analyzing the emotional level of a difficult conversation is to manage the other person's emotions. In almost every difficult conversation, a manager will have to communicate a message that the listener won't like. This can trigger all sorts of negative emotions. And people can't respond effectively when they're upset.

Acknowledge that the other person may feel differently about the conversation than you do. Try to anticipate the reaction when you raise issues. You should expect that the person will ask questions and raise objections to how the conversation is making her feel.

When dealing with other people's emotions, it's important to try to understand their feelings. Prepare to respond to those emotions with some expression of empathic understanding – for example "I understand that you're upset" or "I know this is difficult."

Remember that understanding isn't the same as agreement. You can acknowledge how people feel without approving of their behavior, validating their opinions, or accepting responsibility for their distress.

Now that Rajat has dealt with his own emotions, he's ready to prepare to manage Katherine's emotions.

Select each guideline for analyzing the emotional level of a difficult conversation for an example of how Rajat prepared for his conversation with Katherine.

Anticipate reaction

Rajat considers how he might present the issue to Katherine and anticipates how she might respond. He

Managing Difficult Conversations

doesn't know her motives for taking the laptop, so he imagines what her emotions might be. Katherine could feel angry at him if she thinks she's being accused of theft. She might be frightened of losing her job. Or she could be embarrassed that she inadvertently broke the rules.

Acknowledge feelings

Once Rajat has imagined how Katherine might feel, he thinks about his response. He realizes that no matter what Katherine's motives were, his objective for the conversation is to stay calm and acknowledge Katherine's feelings by demonstrating empathy for her.

Question

What are the guidelines for analyzing the emotional level of a difficult conversation?

Options:

1. Name your emotions
2. Find your emotional middle ground
3. Acknowledge the other person's feelings
4. Anticipate the other person's reaction to the conversation
5. Plan to take responsibility for the other person's distress
6. Prepare to diffuse an emotional response by expressing agreement with the other person's view

Answer:

Option 1: This option is correct. Naming your emotions will help determine that they're authentic emotions, rather than judgments or attributions.

Option 2: This option is correct. Starting in the middle will allow you to either step back or move forward in sharing your emotions during the conversation.

Option 3: This option is correct. Being empathic can show the other person that you understand his feelings.

Option 4: This option is correct. Good preparation involves accepting that the other person may feel differently about the conversation and trying to anticipate the reaction.

Option 5: This option is incorrect. Being empathic and understanding doesn't mean taking responsibility for the other person's reaction to the conversation.

Option 6: This option is incorrect. The right response is to show empathy. You don't have to accept or agree with the other person's side of the issue.

IDENTIFYING THE GOAL

Identifying the goal

The third stage in preparing for a difficult conversation is to identify your goal. If you define your goal in advance, you can stay focused on the reason for the conversation. This means you need to clearly identify what you want to accomplish.

However, you need to be prepared for the fact that there may be some negotiation and compromise involved in achieving your goal. To prepare for negotiation, think about what compromises and changes you might agree to and what won't be acceptable. Then consider the possible consequences of following different conversational paths.

PLANNING THE CONVERSATION

Planning the conversation

The fourth stage in preparing for a difficult conversation is to plan the conversation. Difficult conversations can be stressful and even unpleasant. This means some managers avoid having difficult conversations until forced to deal with the matter, and then go into the situation ill-prepared. Before you have a conversation, it's important to outline the structure of the conversation, and rehearse your approach to achieving your goal.

If you want to achieve your goal, you'll need to devise a strategy for reaching it. This means planning the structure of the conversation.

You'll need to outline the structure by noting the things you need to talk about, and why they're important. Establish a starting point for the discussion. Then create milestones based on the objectives you need to achieve along the way to meeting your goal.

Another important part of planning is to rehearse your approach. Envision your strategic path and where it might go off track. Rehearsing out loud or practicing with a colleague can help refine your technique and increase your resilience to emotion.

Rajat is almost finished preparing for his conversation with Katherine. The final stages are identifying his goal, and planning the conversation.

See each stage for an example of how Rajat prepared for his conversation with Katherine.

Identifying the goal

Rajat considers what he wants to achieve by talking to Katherine. He determines his goal will be to find out why Katherine took the laptop and prevent the problem from reoccurring. He considers how he's going to approach reaching that goal.

Planning the conversation

Rajat plans out a structure for the conversation, deciding when to introduce the subject of the laptop, and how he'll move through the conversation. Then Rajat rehearses his conversation, imagining several different scenarios based on different answers Katherine might give him.

Case Study: Question 1 of 2
Scenario

Remember real estate manager Mai? She's preparing to talk to Lincoln, one of her direct reports. Mai is displeased that Lincoln used her as a reference for an internal position he applied for within the company without asking her first. Mai is almost finished preparing for her difficult conversation with Lincoln.

Answer the questions in order.

Question:

What are examples of Mai analyzing the emotional level of preparing a difficult conversation?

Options:

1. Mai wonders if her feelings are based on resentment that Lincoln didn't consult her before using her as a reference
2. Mai tries to anticipate how Lincoln will react when she raises the issue
3. Mai makes sure to stick to facts and direct observations in preparing her approach
4. Mai plans to let Lincoln know that she's upset he didn't ask before he used her as a reference

Answer:

Option 1: This option is correct. Acknowledging and naming her feelings will help Mai manage her emotions.

Option 2: This option is correct. Anticipating his emotional reactions will help Mai manage Lincoln's feelings.

Option 3: This option is incorrect. Sticking to facts and observations is part of a practical analysis.

Option 4: This option is incorrect. Mai's plan to become emotional with Lincoln could make him defensive.

Case Study: Question 2 of 2

What are examples of Mai planning her approach to a difficult conversation?

Options:

1. Mai drafts a strategy for progressing through to her goal
2. Mai rehearses the conversation with a colleague
3. Mai determines her goal is to tell Lincoln he's not ready for management
4. Mai decides to start the conversation by expressing her hurt and annoyance

5. Mai assumes Lincoln thought she wouldn't find out about the recommendation

Answer:

Option 1: This option is correct. Planning the conversation involves outlining the things you need to talk about, and why they're important.

Option 2: This option is correct. Rehearsing the conversation will help Mai refine her conversational technique.

Option 3: This option is correct. By identifying the goal, Mai will determine the purpose for having the conversation.

Option 4: This option is incorrect. Mai should be concentrating on the purpose of the conversation, not unproductive emotion.

Option 5: This option is incorrect. Mai shouldn't assume she knows Lincoln's intentions.

THE APPROPRIATE MIND-SET

The appropriate mind-set

Mediating disputes, delivering bad news, talking about performance, and counseling employees are all part of being an effective leader. But these difficult conversations can be risky for managers who don't have the right mind-set. It's important to prepare what you're going to communicate by analyzing the practical and emotional levels, setting a clear goal, and planning a strategic path. But it's just as important to prepare how you're going to communicate by examining your own attitude toward the conversation.

So what is a mind-set? It's the logical thinking that determines how you interpret and respond to communication. You need the appropriate mind-set if you're going to communicate effectively in a difficult conversation. This means not only managing your emotions but using them to your advantage.

An appropriate mind-set will help you communicate more effectively during a difficult conversation. The four qualities of an appropriate mind-set are being open-minded, collaborative, empathic, and engaged with the conversation.

See each quality for more information.

Open-minded

Being open-minded means not playing the "blame game." Don't approach the conversation from the perspective of who's right and who's wrong. Other people will respond to you if you listen to their side. Give them the benefit of the doubt, and don't assume the worst about their intentions.

Collaborative

Dictating your own solution can engender resistance in the listener. Being collaborative means offering the other person a role in managing the issue being discussed. Collaboration is about seeking input and listening to the individual's ideas and opinions with honesty and respect.

Empathic

Empathy is the ability to understand what people are feeling, and how the situation looks from their perspective. Being empathic helps you create a bond with the other person, even when you're dealing with a particularly uncomfortable or confrontational conversation.

Engaged

Your ability to be persuasive is greater if you're truly engaged in a conversation. This means actively listening to other people. It also means showing that you're truly interested in what they have to say, and that you care about reaching a positive solution.

Question

Which are qualities of an appropriate mind-set for approaching a difficult conversation?

Options:

1. Open-minded about the other person's perspective 2. Collaborative in reaching a solution

3. Empathic to the other person's feelings

4. Engaged in the conversation

5. Clear about your own solution to the issue 6. Wary of the other person's motives

Answer:

Option 1: This option is correct. It's not productive to approach the conversation from the perspective of who's right and who's wrong.

Option 2: This option is correct. Not paying attention to the other person's view can cause resistance to finding a solution.

Option 3: This option is correct. By showing an understanding of other people's feelings and motives, you can create a bond with them.

Option 4: This option is correct. You'll be more persuasive if you're truly engaged in the conversation.

Option 5: This option is incorrect. An appropriate mind-set involves being collaborative in reaching a solution.

Option 6: This option is incorrect. Being open-minded and empathic will contribute more to a positive attitude than will suspicion.

DEMONSTRATING AN APPROPRIATE MIND-SET

Demonstrating an appropriate mind-set

You can't predict exactly how a difficult conversation will unfold. But an appropriate mind-set can help you choose the appropriate words, tone, and responses to steer the discussion in the right direction. Your conversation should reflect each of the four qualities of an appropriate mind-set – being open-minded, collaborative, empathic, and engaged.

You can show you're open-minded by using neutral language when you're discussing the issue. Instead of affixing blame, present the facts. For example, you could say "This is what I know so far," "This is how the issue was related to me," or "I may not have the story straight, but..."

When you approach the conversation, express yourself without censure or judgment. For example, you might say "I'm not judging you" or "I'm willing to listen to what you have to say."

Make sure to listen to the other person. To keep the conversation on a productive track you could phrase responses in terms of your goal. If someone says "That's not my fault" you might respond "The change needed is..." or "What I'd like to see happen..."

A collaborative approach creates the opportunity for the other person to help you reach your goal. This means you should be ready to relinquish some control over the conversation.

Plan to use diplomatic – not accusatory – language to present the issue. Acknowledge that the other person may have a different perspective than you do.

You should always share your reasoning for having the conversation, and then allow time for a response.

A collaborative approach uses certain statements and questions that are phrased to include the other person:

- How do you feel about what happened?
- What would you say precipitated this issue?
- What do you think you could do to prevent this from happening again?

Question

Which statements demonstrate being open-minded and collaborative?

Options:

1. "I'll tell you what I know about the issue so far."
2. "What do you think you could do differently to prevent this from happening again?
3. "You have to take responsibility for causing this problem."
4. "Just sit and listen to what I have to say."

Answer:

Managing Difficult Conversations

Option 1: This option is correct. Open-minded statements present the facts without affixing blame.

Option 2: This option is correct. Collaborative statements include the other person.

Option 3: This option is incorrect. Blaming someone doesn't demonstrate being open-minded or collaborative.

Option 4: This option is incorrect. Being open-minded and collaborative involves listening to the other person.

Being empathic can help you deal with your own emotions and those of the other person. When you're planning your approach, imagine the stressors the person might experience and how you might respond compassionately. Think about what it might be like to be on the receiving end of your message.

Empathic statements relate primarily to emotions – what you're feeling and what you perceive is going on with the other person. Remember that you don't need to validate the other person's emotions – just simply acknowledge you understand.

You can also create empathy by sharing your own discomfort – particularly if you're relaying bad news. For example, you could say "I'm sorry you didn't get the job" or "I hate to have to tell you this."

Empathic statements involve creating an emotional connection between "I" and "you." For example, you could say "I can understand this is disappointing for you", "I think you're probably feeling a little shocked", or "I feel badly about having to bring this up to you."

An appropriate mind-set also includes being engaged in the conversation. If you're engaged, you're more likely to elicit cooperation from the other person, even when dealing with uncomfortable and confrontational issues.

You can demonstrate engagement by taking time to listen to the other person, and acknowledging what is said. Indicating you're listening can be as simple as indicating understanding. For example, you might show acknowledgment with a gesture, or by using an interjection such as "I see."

You can also show engagement by rephrasing what was just said to show you understand – for example "If I understand what you've just said..." or "It seems like what you're saying is that..."

Question

Tam is the office manager for a high-profile law firm. His coworker Annika has a habit of using expletives and other inappropriate language in the workplace. She thinks it's humorous, but Tam is concerned it could cause offense if overheard by his superiors or by clients.

Match each quality of an appropriate mind-set to how it might be reflected in a conversation. Not all statements may have a match.

Options:

A. Open-minded
B. Collaborative
C. Empathic
D. Engaged

Targets:

1. "This conversation isn't about who's right and who's wrong."

2. "So what do you think you can do to make sure no one is offended?"

3. "I really do understand how this must make you feel."

4. "So what you're saying is that this wasn't intentional. Is that correct?"

5. "You're absolutely right to feel that way."

Answer:

Being open-minded means not judging right and wrong.

Being collaborative means creating the opportunity for the other person to help you reach the goal of the conversation.

Being empathic means relating your own emotions to those of the other person.

Being engaged in the conversation means listening and demonstrating an understanding of what was said.

An appropriate mind-set doesn't mean you must agree with or validate the other person's feelings. Instead, focus on showing empathy and understanding.

RECOGNIZING THE MIND-SET

Recognizing the mind-set

Remember that your conversation should reflect each of the four qualities of an appropriate mind-set – being open-minded, collaborative, empathic, and engaged.

Wilson is the editor-in-chief for a large national newspaper. René is one of his reporters. A colleague of Wilson's has reported to him that René is moonlighting part-time for a competing newspaper. This is a clear-cut conflict of interest. Wilson decides that he needs to have a conversation with René and get him to give up the part-time job. Follow along as Wilson discusses the issue with René.

Wilson: Thanks for meeting with me. We need to talk.
Wilson is concerned.
René: Sure, what's up?
René is friendly.
Wilson: A colleague mentioned that you've been doing some reporting for one of our rivals.
Wilson is concerned.
René: Yeah. Why?

René is suspicious.
Wilson: Well, it's simple. You're full-time here. Working for the competition is wrong and it violates the non-compete agreement you signed when you joined us.
Wilson is firm.
René: But I don't have a choice! I have a student loan to pay off. I need the money.
René is defensive.
Wilson: I understand. That can be stressful. Let's hear your side.
Wilson is sincere.
René: I'm not working on the actual newspaper, I'm writing copy for the web site.
René is defensive.
Wilson: I see. So you thought it was OK to work for the other paper because it was just the online version. You believed you weren't violating the non-compete clause. Have I got that right?
Wilson is professional.
René: Yeah.
René is mollified.
Wilson: I'm sorry, I can see how you might think that, but working for a competitor is a conflict of interest, regardless of the medium. So how are we going to resolve this?
Wilson is sincere.
René: I suppose I'll have to find a different part-time job.
René is accepting.
Wilson achieved his goal for the conversation and demonstrated several of the qualities of an appropriate mind-set. He was collaborative when he invited René to

suggest a solution. He was empathic when he listened to René's reasoning. And he showed he was engaged by listening and repeating back his understanding of the situation. However, Wilson should have been more open-minded and less harsh in his initial choice of words. He told René that working for the competition was wrong. He was right but difficult conversations should focus on a solution, not on blame.

QUALITIES OF AN APPROPRIATE MIND-SET

Qualities of an appropriate mind-set
Case Study: Question 1 of 2
Scenario

You're a senior manager at a large insurance company. One of the company's important clients has complained to you that Greta, one of your direct reports, was extremely rude and disrespectful to him.

You decide to speak to Greta.

Answer the questions about identifying the qualities of an appropriate mind-set for a difficult conversation.

Question:

You're beginning your conversation with Greta.

Identify examples of statements that demonstrate you have the appropriate mind-set for a difficult conversation.

Options:

1. "All I know is the client says you called him a jerk. So tell me your side of the story."

2. "I know this must be difficult for you to hear, but we've had a complaint about your behavior toward a client."

3. "I know what's been going on. You didn't get the sale and now you're angry."

4. "You shouldn't have spoken that way to a client under any circumstances."

5. "I'm here to listen."

Answer:

Option 1: This option is correct. Presenting the facts and not affixing blame shows you're open-minded.

Option 2: This option is correct. You're being empathic by understanding Greta's discomfort and emotions.

Option 3: This option is incorrect. You should keep an open mind and listen to what Greta has to say about her feelings and motives.

Option 4: This option is incorrect. Affixing blame isn't appropriate.

Option 5: This option is correct. Listening is a sign you're engaged in the conversation.

Case Study: Question 2 of 2

You're a senior manager at a large insurance company. One of the company's important clients has complained to you that Greta, one of your direct reports, was extremely rude and disrespectful to him.

You decide to speak to Greta.

Answer the questions about identifying the qualities of an appropriate mind-set for a difficult conversation.

Question:

The conversation is drawing to an end. Greta is explaining that her reaction was due to a suggestive comment made by the client.

Managing Difficult Conversations

Identify examples of statements that demonstrate you have the appropriate mind-set for a difficult conversation.

Options:

1. "I see."
2. "How do you see resolving this situation?"
3. "I want you to apologize, even if you don't mean it."
4. "You were absolutely right. He deserved to be called that name."
5. "I'm very sorry that this happened to you."

Answer:

Option 1: This option is correct. You're demonstrating engagement by listening to Greta and simply acknowledging what she says.

Option 2: This option is correct. You're being collaborative by including Greta in reaching a solution.

Option 3: This option is incorrect. You should be collaborative, not dictatorial if you want Greta's cooperation.

Option 4: This option is incorrect. While you can show empathy and acknowledge how Greta may have felt, you should focus on working toward a solution, not affixing blame.

Option 5: This option is correct. Expressing your own emotions is a sign of being empathic.

HAVING A DIFFICULT CONVERSATION

Having a Difficult Conversation

Have you ever had a difficult conversation with your manager, a direct report, or a colleague? Conversations dealing with difficult topics are common in the work environment. Regardless of your position in an organization, having such conversations is likely to be an uncomfortable part of your job.

You may have noted that a benefit of knowing how to have a difficult conversation is knowing how to approach the conversation better. Knowing how and where it should go will make you feel more comfortable and confident. You'll also develop the appropriate communication style for the conversation.

To achieve a positive resolution you should guide the dialogue through five steps:

1. open with an agenda to define the context of the meeting
2. invite dialogue to connect with the other person

Managing Difficult Conversations

     3. share views and perspectives and be open to learning from each other
     4. look for a mutual understanding of the situation, and
     5. mutually design an action plan

You should be in the right mindset to approach the conversation. Ideally, you'll approach the conversation with an open mind, and remain open-minded for the entire conversation. To achieve this, you should steer the conversation away from who's right or wrong, and avoid attributing blame and thinking competitively – that is, you shouldn't think you have to "win" the conversation.

It's important to use the appropriate communication style from the very beginning. Opening with an agenda means clearly outlining the points that will be discussed and the sequence in which they'll be discussed. Consider Emily, a human resources manager for a large organization. Emily is managing the company's resource planning for the coming year and she's anticipating a difficult conversation with one of the managers, Laura, who hasn't followed the appropriate guidelines.

You can successfully create progress in a difficult conversation using five steps. First, open with an agenda, then invite dialogue. Once you've engaged the other person, you can share views and perspectives. You can then look for a mutual understanding of the situation and design an action plan. You'll then achieve your desired outcome, while still preserving the other person's dignity.

Using weakness-focused communication in conversations threatens the other person. When people feel this way, they often react defensively. So when inviting dialogue, it's important to avoid pointing out the other person's faults or trying to correct them.

Once you've invited the other person to dialogue, you should share views and come to a common understanding. These are the third and fourth steps to making progress in difficult conversations. It's important to not only share your views, but to allow the other person to share also. This exchange of views can be the difference between a positive and negative outcome.

Achieving a successful outcome requires taking all five steps to creating progress in difficult conversations. When you've opened with an agenda, invited dialogue, and shared your views, you're much more likely to reach a mutual understanding of any situation. Once that understanding is achieved, you'll be able to design an action plan to resolve the issue.

When you enter into a difficult conversation, there are five steps you can take to achieve your desired outcome. First, open with an agenda, then invite dialogue using strength-focused communication. Once you've engaged your colleague, you can share your views. You'll then be able to look for a mutual understanding of the situation and design an action plan.

A DIFFICULT CONVERSATION IN ACTION

A difficult conversation in action

Have you ever had a difficult conversation with your manager, a direct report, or a colleague? Conversations dealing with difficult topics are common in the work environment. Regardless of your position in an organization, having such conversations is likely to be an uncomfortable part of your job.

Consider Mike, a bank manager. He's about to have a difficult conversation with Sandra, a member of his team. Sandra has had a lot of upheaval in her personal life, and Mike has given her some personal time and allowed her to leave early on occasion. However, Mike has recently received complaints that Sandra has snapped at colleagues and isn't completing her tasks on time.

Mike has thought about how to approach the conversation; he wants to be fair to Sandra, given her circumstances, but he needs to get commitment from her that she'll refocus and improve her performance. Follow along as Mike discusses the issue with Sandra.

Mike: So, I want to talk about a situation we have brewing.
Mike is cautious.
Sandra: Oh? What's up?
Sandra is curious.
Mike: Look, I know you've had a tough time lately...I get that. But...well...it seems like you're not pulling your weight on the team.
Mike is careful.
Sandra: What are you talking about? Who said that?
Sandra is surprised.
Mike: There have been some complaints...
Mike is hesitant.
Sandra: About me? Who's complaining about me?
Sandra is alarmed.
Mike: I'd rather not say.
Mike is cautious.
Sandra: Well, can you at least tell me what the complaint was about?
Sandra is concerned.
Mike: OK, well...let's start with your attitude...
Mike is careful.
Sandra: My attitude? I don't think I have an attitude.
Sandra is confused.
Mike: Try not to get upset. Like I said, I know you've had a tough time lately...
Mike is defensive.
Sandra: I don't understand...what is the problem? Have I upset somebody?
Sandra is careful.
Mike: No...it's not that...
Mike is awkward.

Sandra: Is it about the client issue yesterday? Listen, I can explain...
Sandra is frantic.
Mike: Oh...OK, good. Why don't we start there?
Mike is relieved.

Mike went into the meeting with Sandra feeling he was prepared. He knew his desired outcome, but wanted to show empathy to Sandra. He also wanted to show that he respects her and understands that her circumstances are difficult. However, the conversation didn't progress as Mike had planned. Sandra became upset and reacted emotionally.

Even though Mike prepared well for the meeting, he opened the conversation poorly and was unable to keep the conversation focused. Subsequently, he allowed Sandra to take control of the conversation by giving her the opportunity to discuss another issue.

So why did Mike's conversation go so wrong? One reason is because Mike didn't know how the conversation should unfold. His lack of structure caused the conversation to lose focus. Mike needed to clearly outline the reason for the meeting.

Another reason for the failure of the conversation is that Mike's communication style didn't allow him to keep the conversation open and focused. If he'd been more clear and direct, and presented his views assertively, he may have achieved his desired outcome of gaining commitment from Sandra to improve her performance in a tactful way.

BENEFITS FROM DIFFICULT CONVERSATIONS

Benefits from difficult conversations

You may have noted that a benefit of knowing how to have a difficult conversation is knowing how to approach the conversation better. Knowing how and where it should go will make you feel more comfortable and confident. You'll also develop the appropriate communication style for the conversation.

Having a clear structure for the conversation and knowing the different steps you should take will also give you a better idea of how you'll achieve your desired outcomes.

Finally, you'll be better equipped to evaluate the progress of the situation. Based on this evaluation, you'll be able to take the next step to make the conversation progress.

There are many benefits from learning how to have a difficult conversation. If you know the steps to take to make progress during the conversation and develop an appropriate communication style, the conversation is likely to become a learning experience for both parties.

STEPS TO CONDUCT DIFFICULT CONVERSATIONS

Steps to conduct difficult conversations

To achieve a positive resolution you should guide the dialogue through five steps:
1. open with an agenda to define the context of the meeting
2. invite dialogue to connect with the other person
3. share views and perspectives and be open to learning from each other
4. look for a mutual understanding of the situation, and
5. mutually design an action plan

See each step, in order, to learn more about it.

1. Open with an agenda

Having an agenda has two purposes. It helps you clearly plan the meeting in advance, and it also helps you keep the meeting on track. So if you find the conversation going off on a tangent, you can use the agenda to refocus the conversation.

A good agenda outlines the problem to be discussed and establishes a time to hear your colleague's views. It also allows you time to present your views, and invites you and the colleague to take a collaborative approach to resolving the issue.

2. Invite dialogue

You want to create an atmosphere that invites dialogue. At this stage, it's important to connect with the other person.

3. Share views and perspectives

You need to share your views with a focus on the facts, and not present your perspective as a "one and only" stance. It's important for you to hear your colleague's views and perspectives, so ask for them. Then you should listen carefully and try to avoid judging your colleague. And be aware of your own assumptions, the most basic of which is that you're right and your colleague is wrong.

4. Look for a mutual understanding

It's important that both parties are involved in the resolution process. Rather than dictate the solution, it's a good idea to first invite your colleague to propose potential solutions. If your colleague makes a contribution to the solution, it's easier to reach a mutual understanding.

5. Design an action plan

An action plan formally clarifies the understanding that's been reached by both parties. It also identifies "next steps," and who's responsible for each activity. The action plan should be written down and agreed upon by both parties. A clear action plan helps avoid misunderstandings about who's responsible for each task. There should also be agreement on the time lines associated with the plan.

Consider Anna, a team leader at an insurance company. She's preparing for a difficult conversation with Peter, a member of her team. Peter's performance has been below average for several months now. Anna finds this surprising, since Peter has worked for the company for six years and always performed well in the past. Anna's desired outcome is to find the cause of Peter's change in behavior, and to determine the steps to improve his performance.

Anna has thought about her approach to the conversation, and she starts by presenting an agenda. She first wants to hear Peter's feedback and then discuss three recent incidents of missed deadlines and work through them with him.

When asked for his feedback, Peter says that he often feels overwhelmed by the workload, and that he's underresourced. Anna then presents the three incidents she wants to discuss and asks Peter to pinpoint where his challenges are. Peter says he feels unable to ask for help from others.

She then asks for Peter's suggestions to overcome the problem. Anna agrees that reprioritizing certain tasks is a good way to address the issue and states that it could be implemented immediately.

Question

You're bracing for a stressful interaction with a difficult colleague. Place the five steps that create progress in a difficult conversation in order.

Options:
A. Open with an agenda
B. Invite dialogue
C. Share views and perspectives

D. Look for a mutual understanding
E. Mutually design an action plan

Answer:

Open with an agenda is ranked the first step to create progress. This is the first step in making progress in a difficult conversation. Without an agenda, it's difficult to structure the conversation and keep your colleague focused on the issue.

Invite dialogue is ranked the second step to create progress. This is the second step in making progress in a difficult conversation. You should present the facts in an objective manner that invites a collaborative approach to solving the issue.

Share views and perspectives is ranked the third step to create progress. This is the third step in making progress in a difficult conversation. It's important for you to listen carefully and hear your colleague's version of events.

Look for a mutual understanding is ranked the fourth step to create progress. This is the fourth step in making progress in a difficult conversation. You and your colleague should work together to resolve the issue.

Mutually design an action plan is ranked the fifth step to create progress. This is the fifth step in making progress in a difficult conversation. An action plan should be formally written down with time frames attached to it.

APPROACHING DIFFICULT CONVERSATIONS

Approaching difficult conversations

You should be in the right mindset to approach the conversation. Ideally, you'll approach the conversation with an open mind, and remain open-minded for the entire conversation. To achieve this, you should steer the conversation away from who's right or wrong, and avoid attributing blame and thinking competitively – that is, you shouldn't think you have to "win" the conversation.

You should also approach the conversation with curiosity and view the situation as an opportunity to learn. If you take a collaborative approach, you'll be more likely to avoid blaming the other person or thinking competitively. Being willing to engage in a collaborative way allows you to take time to understand the situation from all perspectives.

Empathy toward your colleague will also help progress the conversation positively. Considering your colleague's emotional state and feelings will help demonstrate respect.

Managing Difficult Conversations

When approaching the conversation with this frame of mind, you help preserve the dignity of your colleague. For a successful outcome to the meeting, this frame of mind must prevail throughout the entire conversation.

Your communication style should convey that you have a positive mindset. An appropriate communication style involves being clear and direct with your colleague, and being honest and fair with your views. Listen effectively to what your colleague has to say, and be assertive but tactful. It's also important to keep the focus on the facts at all times.

See each characteristic to learn more about it.

Clear and direct

You need to be clear and direct when talking to a colleague about a difficult subject. It's important that you don't go off on tangents, attribute blame, or talk around the subject. Instead, have a good plan to keep you focused on the agenda.

Honest and fair

Presenting information honestly means focusing on the facts. Be careful of your assumptions as they may cause you to view a situation subjectively, and can cause an unsatisfactory end to a conversation. Typical assumptions include "I'm right," "He's wrong," "There's no other explanation," or perhaps "She doesn't know what she's talking about."

Remember, you probably don't really know what your colleague's thinking, so be fair. Identify your assumptions, put them aside, and give your colleague the benefit of the doubt.

Listen effectively

When you have a clear idea of what a problem is, and you're clear about its remedy, it's often difficult to be swayed otherwise. One of the most important skills in dialogue – if not the most important skill – is listening.

Listening involves being open-minded enough to see that there may be another perspective to the situation that you haven't considered. Listening therefore requires openness, respect for your colleague, adaptability, and a bit of modesty.

To demonstrate effective listening, you should ask your colleague open-ended questions and listen carefully to the answers. This will help you avoid misunderstandings and make the other person feel heard. Furthermore, a good listener is less likely to cause the other person to become unnecessarily upset.

Be assertive but tactful

Assertiveness shouldn't be confused with aggressiveness. Being assertive means stating the facts in an objective way, and being prepared for a possible negative response from your colleague. It requires confidence, conviction, and taking responsibility for your opinions and actions. You should always come across as calm – not aggressive – to the other person.

Tact is being sensitive to the other person's feelings. You can be assertive, yet still get the facts – and your views – across in a thoughtful and diplomatic way.

Keep the focus on facts

Keep the focus on the facts, but also be aware that there may be different interpretations of the facts. Focusing on the facts can help you avoid having the conversation turn emotional. Present the main points and go into detail as required. Prior to the meeting, consider how the facts could possibly be misinterpreted by others.

To help keep you focused on the relevant facts, you should avoid giving unsolicited advice. Also, try not to act patronizing or sarcastic, and steer clear of making ambiguous insinuations.

OPENING A DIFFICULT CONVERSATION

Opening a difficult conversation

It's important to use the appropriate communication style from the very beginning. Opening with an agenda means clearly outlining the points that will be discussed and the sequence in which they'll be discussed. Consider Emily, a human resources manager for a large organization. Emily is managing the company's resource planning for the coming year and she's anticipating a difficult conversation with one of the managers, Laura, who hasn't followed the appropriate guidelines.

As Emily prepares her agenda, she thinks about the correct approach for communicating her concerns to Laura. She approaches the conversation with an open mind. Emily doesn't want to assume Laura was negligent by not following the guidelines. She also doesn't want to blame Laura for adding to her considerable workload by having to revisit her proposal with the senior management team.

Managing Difficult Conversations

Emily understands that Laura is under stress due to managing a growing department. She's also curious about Laura's approach to the proposal, and considers that she may not have all the facts. Emily is now meeting with Laura. Follow along as she discusses the resource planning issue with Laura.

Emily: So, you saw my e-mail. Let's talk about your resource allocation proposal.
Emily is calm.
Laura: OK.
Laura is calm.
Emily: You've got the agenda?
Emily is calm.
Laura: Yes, I have it here.
Laura is calm, and gestures to the folder in front of her.
Emily: So, I'd like to hear your thoughts, and see how to bring your proposal in line with the others. Does that work for you?
Emily is calm.
Laura: Absolutely.
Laura is calm.
Emily: Great! So...from what I can see, you've followed your own process. Not the one agreed at the senior management meeting. Correct?
Emily is calm.
Laura: Yes, I did what made sense to me.
Laura is calm.
Emily: OK. So, what's your take on the resource planning guidelines?
Emily is calm.
Laura: Well, I'm glad you asked...
Laura is intent.

Emily opened the conversation well. She was clear and direct about the desired outcome of the meeting by discussing the agenda. She focused on the facts rather than implying any wrongdoing on Laura's part. As such, Emily communicated assertively, but she was also tactful by not assigning blame to Laura.

Emily conveyed effective listening skills, both in her actions and her demeanor. She allowed Laura to speak without interrupting, and gave Laura her full attention. Overall, Emily's approach was both honest and fair toward Laura.

IDENTIFYING APPROPRIATE CHARACTERISTICS

Identifying appropriate characteristics
Question
Which characteristics are appropriate when communicating with others in difficult conversations?
Options:
1. Being clear and direct about the facts
2. Being assertive but tactful
3. Listening effectively
4. Being adamant about your personal views
5. Interpreting the facts

Answer:
Option 1: This option is correct. Being clear and direct in a difficult conversation is important. It helps keep the conversation focused, and helps avoid the other person going off on tangents.

Option 2: This option is correct. You should always calmly and tactfully state the facts in a difficult conversation. Assertiveness requires confidence, conviction, and taking responsibility for your opinions and actions.

Option 3: This option is correct. Listening effectively is one of the most important skills in dialogue. It's particularly important in difficult conversations to avoid misunderstandings.

Option 4: This option is incorrect. It's not appropriate to be stubborn or inflexible about your subjective views. You should be assertive and tactful, and listen carefully.

Option 5: This option is incorrect. It's always best to be honest and fair with the facts. Any attempt to skew the facts may appear deceitful.

INVITING DIALOGUE

Inviting dialogue

You can successfully create progress in a difficult conversation using five steps. First, open with an agenda, then invite dialogue. Once you've engaged the other person, you can share views and perspectives. You can then look for a mutual understanding of the situation and design an action plan. You'll then achieve your desired outcome, while still preserving the other person's dignity.

Inviting dialogue is the second step to progressing difficult conversations. Your aim is to fully engage your colleague. You need to connect in order to work together toward a positive outcome – regardless of whether the outcome is an improvement in performance, a change in behavior, or relationship building. Inviting dialogue in a positive manner helps create an environment of trust.

To connect with your colleague, you need to use the appropriate communication style. In particular, you need to use strength-focused communication, rather than weakness-focused communication.

See each communication style to learn more.

Strength-focused communication

Strength-focused communication involves focusing on the other person's strengths, even in difficult situations. This can be challenging because sometimes it's hard to understand a colleague's negative behavior. It can be even harder to show empathy and listen effectively.

Although it may be challenging, using strength-focused communication is key to inviting dialogue. It can help keep the other person engaged in working toward a solution.

Weakness-focused communication

Weakness-focused communication causes dialogue to fail because one person is pointing out perceived weaknesses in the other. It often manifests as open criticism. Focusing on a person's weaknesses doesn't work because people tend to react negatively to criticism, even if the comments are justified.

Weakness-focused communication prevents you from connecting because your colleague will be less open to listening to what you have to say. So it's very unlikely to change your colleague's behavior.

USING WEAKNESS-FOCUSED COMMUNICATION

Using weakness-focused communication

Using weakness-focused communication in conversations threatens the other person. When people feel this way, they often react defensively. So when inviting dialogue, it's important to avoid pointing out the other person's faults or trying to correct them.

Consider Andrew. He's a team leader with a client services team. Andrew overhears one of this team members, Noah, being abrupt and sarcastic toward a client on the phone. Noah is usually calm, and it's out of character for him to be anything but professional. Follow along as Andrew addresses the issue with Noah.

Andrew: Noah, I need to talk to you.

Andrew is annoyed.

Noah: (Look, I'll call you back.) Sure, what's up?

Noah ends his phone call and addresses Andrew calmly.

Andrew: What do you think? Your run in with Sophie!

Andrew is annoyed.

Noah: Huh, she's such a pain!
Noah is frustrated.
Andrew: You really shouldn't have spoken to her that way.
Andrew is annoyed.
Noah: Excuse me?
Noah is surprised.
Andrew: You practically yelled at her!
Andrew is annoyed.
Noah: But let me explain what happened...
Noah is defensive.
Andrew: I really don't care. She's a client!
Andrew is annoyed.
Noah: But, at least hear...
Noah interrupts.
Andrew: Listen to me! I don't want it to happen again. OK?
Andrew interrupts.
Noah: You don't even know what actually happened!
Noah is defensive.
Andrew: It's pretty self-explanatory, Noah. You should call her and apologize.
Andrew is sarcastic.
Noah: Fine...I'll call her...
Noah is defeated.
Andrew: Good.
Andrew is pleased.
Noah: OK...I overreacted. But it would've been nice to have a say here. Anyway, I'll apologize. As you said, she's a client...
Noah is defeated.

Andrew's use of weakness-focused communication made Noah feel threatened. He felt like he was being attacked.

Weakness-focused communication prevented Andrew from connecting with Noah because Noah wasn't open to listening to what he had to say.

USING STRENGTH-FOCUSED COMMUNICATION

Using strength-focused communication

Strength-focused communication involves speaking to a person's strengths, acknowledging feelings and frustrations, and understanding the benefits of a different approach.

See each characteristic to learn more.

Speaking to strengths

Everyone has strengths and weaknesses. So when you speak to a person's strengths, you can leverage those strengths to help resolve a situation. For instance, you can appeal to a person's experience to engage the person to help train new staff.

Acknowledging feelings and frustrations

When you acknowledge feelings and frustrations, coaching or disciplining a direct report will be much more effective. For example, acknowledging someone's feelings can demonstrate empathy and help avoid the other person becoming defensive.

Understanding benefits of approach

Managing Difficult Conversations

When a colleague feels you understand the benefits of a different approach, it becomes much easier for that person to listen to your concerns. For example, recognizing the benefits of a colleague's proposal will establish that you've fully considered any suggestions made.

Consider Emily, a human resources manager for a global organization. Emily is managing the company's resource planning for next year and she's having a difficult conversation with a manager, Laura, who hasn't followed the appropriate guidelines. Emily opened the conversation well, and was clear and direct with the facts. Follow along as Emily and Laura continue to discuss Laura's approach to the proposal.

Emily: I notice you used a different method to work out the estimated new hires for next year. Why?

Emily is calm.

Laura: Yes, that's right. I didn't like the other approach. This one made more sense to me.

Laura is calm.

Emily: I see. It's good that you're aware of the differences. That makes it easier for me to help you amend your proposal.

Emily is calm.

Laura: I could do with the help. I've wasted so much time on it already...

Laura is regretful.

Emily: Don't be hard on yourself! It's great you're thinking of better ways to do things.

Emily is calm.

Laura: Thanks!

Laura is appreciative.

Emily: Look, I know this all seems a bit bureaucratic. But it has to be done this way for transparency.
Emily is regretful.
Laura: It did seem tedious.
Laura is calm.
Emily: Your proposal was interesting, though. Maybe we can use some of your ideas next year.
Emily is calm.
Laura: That would be great!
Laura is calm.

Emily used strength-focused communication in her dialogue with Laura. She acknowledged Laura's feelings and frustrations by showing empathy and explaining the reasons behind the process. This was demonstrated when she said that the process seemed a bit bureaucratic, but it has to be done that way for transparency.

Emily also spoke to Laura's strengths. She managed to find a positive view of Laura's actions, rather than a negative view, by telling her it's great to always be thinking of better ways to do things.

In addition, Emily showed understanding of the benefits of Laura's approach. Emily showed that she'd really considered Laura's point of view when she said the proposal was interesting, and perhaps she'd use some of the ideas next year.

Question

Which invitations to dialogue are examples of using strength-focused communication?

Options:

1. "You're great at training others. Perhaps you could prioritize more effectively if you delegated some tasks?"

Managing Difficult Conversations

2. "I realize that you find it challenging to prioritize tasks in a matrix structure."

3. "I'm glad I've had the opportunity to consider the issue from your perspective."

4. "You shouldn't have treated the customer that way."

5. "I've noticed that you've been arriving 20 minutes late on a regular basis."

6. "I'd like us to sit down and talk. Are you free now, or would it be more convenient during lunchtime?"

Answer:

Option 1: This option is correct. It's important to always speak to the other person's strengths.

Option 2: This option is correct. You'll have more success if you acknowledge the feelings and frustrations of the other person.

Option 3: This option is correct. You should aim to make the other person feel you understand the benefits of her approach.

Option 4: This option is incorrect. Making a statement of judgment isn't an example of strength-focused communication. You should aim to speak to the other person's strengths.

Option 5: This option is incorrect. Although it's important to state the facts, this isn't an example of strength-focused communication. An example would be acknowledging feelings and frustrations.

Option 6: This option is incorrect. Although it's important to find a suitable time to talk, this isn't an example of strength-focused communication. An example would be making someone feel you understand the benefits of another approach.

HOW TO ACHIEVE A MUTUAL UNDERSTANDING

How to achieve a mutual understanding
Once you've invited the other person to dialogue, you should share views and come to a common understanding. These are the third and fourth steps to making progress in difficult conversations. It's important to not only share your views, but to allow the other person to share also. This exchange of views can be the difference between a positive and negative outcome.

There are several helpful guidelines to follow when sharing your views and perspectives:
- prioritize by discussing the most important issues first,
- present the situation with a focus on facts,
- be flexible – don't present your views as one-sided, and
- share all relevant information to support your views.

See each guideline to learn more about it.
Prioritize

To reach a mutual understanding, it's important to say what's most important first. Your priorities should be stated explicitly and objectively. If stated in this way, your colleague should be open to joint problem-solving.

If you tend to leave the main issue to the end of a meeting, you may leave others in a position of uncertainty and frustration that the conversation was one-sided.

Focus on facts

Starting a difficult conversation with the facts helps keep emotions in check and establish an understanding of the issue. Try to avoid getting too personal during the conversation – for instance, by making negative comments about the other person's personality. Instead, engage the other person in problem-solving.

It's best to avoid attributing blame when you discuss the cause of a problem and the people involved. Blaming wastes unnecessary time on the problem rather than finding a solution.

Be flexible

It's important to be flexible in the conversation. Try to avoid presenting your views rigidly. Flexibility requires openness to hearing an alternative point of view.

Listening is particularly important when it comes to being flexible. You can't progress a conversation in a more positive direction unless your colleague feels heard and understood.

Share relevant information

Share any relevant information or reasoning behind your views. It helps to have concrete examples to back up your views. For instance, if you want to discuss frequent lateness, make sure you have concrete examples of the lateness to back up your claims.

Relevant information can include emotions, as unexpressed feelings can inhibit good communication. It's therefore important to identify and understand any emotional blockers that are contributing to an issue.

To come to a mutual understanding of the situation, you should also ask the other person for her views, empathize with her answers, and reframe the facts.

See each guideline to learn more about it.

Ask for views

Don't assume that your views are necessarily "right." It's usually easy to agree on facts; it's the interpretation of facts that can cause conflict. To create progress during a conversation, you need to be curious about the other person's views. So try to understand why your colleague interprets the situation in a particular way.

To successfully ask for views, use open-ended questions and listen carefully to the answers. Avoid statements, hints, or leading questions. It's important to gather all the relevant or missing information before an understanding can be reached.

Empathize and reframe

Acknowledge the significance of your colleague's feelings, and empathize. Avoid assuming that you know how your colleague is feeling. If in doubt, ask. Also, consider that the impact of your colleague's actions or behavior is likely different to the original intent. Ask what your colleague's original intent was, and remain open-minded.

Reframing is a technique for keeping the conversation on the right track, such as paraphrasing what the other person is saying into more constructive concepts. For instance, if a colleague blames someone for a mistake, you could reframe the statements to acknowledge that there were many contributors to the mistake.

The fifth and final step to making progress during difficult conversations is to mutually design an action plan. Formally making a plan will ensure that what was agreed upon in the meeting will be carried out going forward.

Question

Match each dialogue activity to the corresponding step in making progress in difficult conversations. Each step may have more than one match.

Options:

A. Avoid attributing blame
B. Be curious about alternative views of the situation
C. Give concrete examples of the behavior
D. Acknowledge your colleague's feelings

Targets:

1. Share views and perspectives
2. Look for a mutual understanding

Answer:

When sharing views, it's best to avoid attributing blame by focusing on the facts. Giving concrete examples of the behavior can help keep the conversation on track.

Being curious and asking questions can help you learn from the other person and reach an understanding. Acknowledging feelings through empathy helps you consider what your colleague's original intent was.

Even if you follow these guidelines, you could encounter some conversation blockers, such as emotions. Keeping the conversation objective can help you avoid this and engage with a focus on facts. For instance, if you have negative opinions about the person, it's useful prior to the meeting to move from an emotional view of the person to a factual view.

You can use three techniques to view other people more objectively. First, you can view people from their own perspective. For instance, you might think your colleague Sam is demanding, but he may see himself as results-oriented.

Second, you can reduce negative opinions to facts. For example, an emotional view of a colleague, Polly, could be that she's not a team player. You could change this opinion into a factual view – perhaps that Polly has clearly-defined views about her job responsibilities.

The third technique is to find a nobler intention. For example, perhaps you feel a colleague, Simon, is lazy because he's often late delivering reports to you. Instead of accusing Simon of being lazy, you could consider that he may just be a perfectionist.

Question

Consider Janice, a client services manager. She's organized a meeting with Neil, one of her team members, to discuss his recent poor performance. Neil has made several errors on a client account, and Janice feels that he's lazy and uncooperative.

What techniques can Janice use to change her negative opinion?

Options:

1. She can consider how Neil views his attitude to his work
2. She can differentiate between her opinions and the factual details of Neil's performance
3. She can consider what Neil's intentions might be

4. She can calmly share her views on Neil's uncooperative personality

5. She can consider that she may be wrong about Neil's poor performance

Answer:

Janice shouldn't doubt the facts. Neil made errors that need to be addressed. However, it's better for her to avoid focusing on Neil's personality. Techniques for viewing other people objectively include viewing people from their perspective, reducing negative opinions to facts, and finding nobler intentions.

Correct answer(s):

1. She can consider how Neil views his attitude to his work

2. She can differentiate between her opinions and the factual details of Neil's performance

3. She can consider what Neil's intentions might be

ASSESSING A CONVERSATION

Assessing a conversation

Consider Graham, a frontline manager at a retail store. He's in a meeting with Irene, a member of his team. Graham feels that Irene's performance isn't up to his standard of a customer-facing employee. Her sales figures are 50% less than average, and he suspects this is a result of a poor attitude. Follow along as Graham discusses the issue with Irene.

Graham: Irene, let's have a chat about your sales figures.

Graham is calm.

Irene: Sure! What's up?

Irene is happy.

Graham: Well, you know all about sales targets...Do you understand what your targets are?

Graham is calm.

Irene: Yes.

Irene is cautious.

Graham: Good! Well, a typical employee closes 100 sales a week. For you it's more like 40 to 50.

Graham is matter-of-fact.
Irene: Oh really? That's surprising.
Irene is cautious.
Graham: So you see why there's a problem?
Graham is relieved.
Irene: I guess so...
Irene is cautious.
Graham: You have to remember that performance is measured by sales targets...so your job really isn't safe unless this improves significantly...
Graham is uncomfortable.
Irene: But I work really hard! I spend time with the customers, listen to them, and make sure they're happy with their purchases!
Irene is upset.
Graham: But that's not reflected in your sales...
Graham is indignant.
Irene: Well, if you ask me, the others focus too much on targets...whatever happened to customer service?
Irene is upset.
Graham: I think you're missing the point, Irene!
Graham is frustrated.
Irene: I don't think so! It's obvious you think money's more important than service!
Irene is upset.

Graham opened the conversation by prioritizing. He explicitly and objectively explained that sales targets are very important. He also focused on the facts well and shared relevant information to support his views.

However, Graham asked close-ended questions, and didn't empathize with Irene or reframe her views. He also wasn't flexible enough to consider Irene's point of view.

He didn't acknowledge that Irene's focus on client service incorrectly gave the impression that she wasn't working hard enough.

Graham may have achieved a better outcome by asking open-ended questions and demonstrating empathy toward Irene.

ACHIEVING A SUCCESSFUL OUTCOME

Achieving a successful outcome

Achieving a successful outcome requires taking all five steps to creating progress in difficult conversations. When you've opened with an agenda, invited dialogue, and shared your views, you're much more likely to reach a mutual understanding of any situation. Once that understanding is achieved, you'll be able to design an action plan to resolve the issue.

Remember Emily, the HR manager for a global organization? She's discussing the required changes to Laura's resource planning proposal. Emily used strength-focused communication to invite dialogue with Laura. Follow along as Emily and Laura continue their conversation.

Emily: It's important we get your proposal in line with the others ASAP. We've a tight deadline so we need to work together on this. Are you on board?

Emily is matter-of-fact.

Laura: Yeah, but, the problem is, I can't make any sense of these forecasting guidelines. And there's so many "assumptions" we're supposed to make...

Laura is initially hesitant, then frustrated.

Emily: OK, so you're saying that you find the mathematical calculations challenging. And, you don't like the guesswork involved. Is that right?

Emily is calm and focused.

Laura: Yeah, pretty much.

Laura looks defeated.

Emily: I hear you...I don't like math either! So, to start with, let's get you comfortable with the calculations.

Emily is calm and focused.

Laura: Sounds good.

Laura looks hopeful.

Emily: So how do you want to do it?

Emily is calm and focused.

Laura: Well, Bill really helped me get my head around the performance metrics...maybe he can help?

Laura is thoughtful.

Emily: Great! It will also help to look at Sam's proposal. It's a good example.

Emily is calm and focused.

Laura: I'll set up meetings with Bill and Sam and let you know if I've any problems.

Laura is happy.

Emily: Perfect. Can I expect to hear from you by...Friday?

Emily is calm and focused.

Laura: Absolutely!

Laura is calm and focused.

Managing Difficult Conversations

Emily managed a successful outcome in her meeting with Laura. She achieved this by discussing the important issue, focusing on facts, being flexible, sharing relevant information to support her views, asking open-ended questions, and empathizing and reframing.

Once Emily and Laura had a mutual understanding of the situation, they were able to brainstorm ideas and work on an action plan together to address the issue.

THE SITUATION

The situation

When you enter into a difficult conversation, there are five steps you can take to achieve your desired outcome. First, open with an agenda, then invite dialogue using strength-focused communication. Once you've engaged your colleague, you can share your views. You'll then be able to look for a mutual understanding of the situation and design an action plan.

In this topic, you'll get the chance to engage in a difficult conversation with a direct report in a simulated scenario, in which you'll be taking on the role of a new advertising manager for Imagenie, a successful multinational advertising company.

Recently, Claude – one of your direct reports – overpromised and underdelivered to a key client, Diallonics. Diallonics had an order in for brochures to support a new ad campaign they were undertaking and asked for them sooner than the normal four-week turnaround outlined in the Service Level Agreement.

Claude committed to providing the brochures in three weeks.

Due to production conflicts, the brochures weren't ready as promised. The client received the materials in four weeks, per the SLA, but the delay forced them to postpone the start of their ad campaign. As a result, Diallonics threatened to move their business to a competitor.

You looked into the situation and reviewed the correspondence between Claude, the client, and other departments in the company. You conclude that if the client's expectations had been managed according to the Service Level Agreement, the company wouldn't be in this situation.

You've managed to pacify Diallonics for the moment, but your goal with Claude is to ensure he makes realistic promises to clients going forward, in line with company policy.

You also realize you need to give Claude more support and guidance to help him manage expectations more effectively with his clients. Your initial thoughts are to have Claude run his client-related communications by you on a weekly basis so you can coach him on this aspect of his job. However, you don't want him to feel that you're trying to micromanage him.

HANDLING DIFFICULT CONVERSATIONS EFFECTIVELY

Handling Difficult Conversations Effectively

Everyone has experienced a personal conversation that went wrong. This can happen when there are misunderstandings, when people are stressed, or when people dislike each other. In your professional life, conversations can also become difficult. Perhaps you're a manager or supervisor and you need to deal with members of your team or department. These work-based conversations can be very difficult, even if you prepare carefully for them.

During difficult conversations, challenges may emerge when the other person doesn't engage in dialogue, the conversation takes a destructive direction, or you become challenged by your own emotions.

When you deal with a person who won't engage with you, an effective strategy is to comment on the person's reaction and take control of the situation by asking questions. If the person is distracted by something else, make a comment about it. If the person ignores you completely, explain in a neutral tone how this makes you feel. You can use questions to probe the other person's point of view and to prompt justification from the person.

A conversation going in a destructive direction is the second difficult conversation challenge that you may face. The strategy for getting it back on track is to reframe unhelpful statements made by the person you're talking with. You can do this by changing unhelpful statements into helpful ones to facilitate creating progress during the conversation.

One of the most challenging aspects of managing a difficult conversation is to keep the discussion on track. The person you're talking with may not like what you have to say and might try to make the conversation go in a different direction. Very often, that direction may be destructive in nature. Assigning blame, claiming to be right, and making accusations can cause a conversation to go in a destructive direction.

You use the guidelines for reframing a conversation to achieve a successful outcome. By reframing, you help the person you are in conversation with make the transition from assigning blame, claiming to be right, or making accusations to a point where the person is an active contributor to the conversation.

Sometimes, during a difficult conversation, your emotions may get the better of you. You might become frustrated and angry, or you might become upset and withdrawn. These emotions are part of your natural defenses. However, losing control of your emotions won't help you to achieve a successful outcome. In fact, these emotions lead to fight or flight behavior on your part. An angry response is an example of fight behavior, while a defensive response represents flight behavior.

Being criticized is the second trigger that may cause you to experience strong emotions during a difficult conversation. This can also lead you to experience fight or flight reactions, which can jeopardize the conversation.

However, you can handle criticism in a difficult conversation by following a number of steps. First, you need to recognize your own reactions and then listen. Next, you should ask questions. And finally, you respond.

WHEN CONVERSATIONS BECOME DIFFICULT

When conversations become difficult

Everyone has experienced a personal conversation that went wrong. This can happen when there are misunderstandings, when people are stressed, or when people dislike each other. In your professional life, conversations can also become difficult. Perhaps you're a manager or supervisor and you need to deal with members of your team or department. These work-based conversations can be very difficult, even if you prepare carefully for them.

Take Virginia for instance. She's a financial manager with an advertising company. She's preparing to have a conversation with Lucas, an administrative assistant in her department. She has repeatedly asked Lucas to complete simple tasks. But he has failed to complete them. The conversation is going to be difficult because Virginia is asking Lucas to change his behavior.

Virginia prepares for the conversation by making sure she's clear about her feelings before she engages Lucas in conversation. Virginia also tries to anticipate Lucas' reaction so that she's able to manage the conversation effectively. Additionally, Virginia has a clear structure in mind to make the conversation progress toward a constructive outcome.

She plans to open with an agenda, invite dialogue to connect with Lucas, learn and share views and perspectives, look for a mutual understanding of the situation, and mutually design an action plan. Even though Virginia is prepared for the difficult conversation, Lucas can make it even more challenging and difficult, depending on his attitude.

Virginia invites Lucas to the meeting by e-mail. She's included the meeting's agenda in the e-mail. Virginia requested that Lucas compile a list of the tasks he was asked to complete in the past two weeks. Follow along to learn about the challenges she encounters during the conversation.

Virginia: As I mentioned in my e-mail, I'd like to go over the tasks I've asked you to complete over the past two weeks. I want to work with you on a way to improve your overall performance. Are you OK with this agenda?

Virginia is serious.

Lucas: Fine.

Lucas is disinterested.

Virginia: How do you find the tasks you've been assigned lately? Are there any concerns or difficulties you'd like to share? You haven't completed any of your recent assignments.

Virginia is calm.

Lucas: Oh, it's OK for you to blame me for not completing assignments, but how could I complete them when you don't respond to e-mail?
Lucas is spiteful
Virginia: What? This isn't about me. Who do you think you are?
Virginia is angry.
Even though Virginia had prepared for the conversation, it still became difficult. The conversation took a destructive direction when Lucas chose to ignore the issue of his own performance and blame Virginia for causing the problem.

Virginia became challenged by her own emotions and reacted angrily. Her response has jeopardized the possibility of achieving a successful outcome.

CHALLENGES OF DIFFICULT CONVERSATIONS

Challenges of difficult conversations

During difficult conversations, challenges may emerge when the other person doesn't engage in dialogue, the conversation takes a destructive direction, or you become challenged by your own emotions.

See each challenge that you may face during a difficult conversation because of the nature of what is being discussed for more information.

Person doesn't engage

A person who doesn't engage shows no interest in the conversation, despite your best efforts.

Conversation takes a destructive direction

The conversation takes a destructive direction when the other person begins to take a stance that threatens the possibility of achieving a successful outcome.

Challenged by your own emotions

You can be challenged by your own emotions when they get the better of you. Your resulting reaction can jeopardize the conversation.

Managing Difficult Conversations

The first challenge you may face occurs when a person doesn't engage in dialogue. This can be very frustrating for you and equally difficult to manage.

You can't make a connection if the person refuses to meaningfully respond to you. The person you are talking to may be responding with simple answers such as "OK," or "I agree." But you may notice that the individual is paying more attention to what's going on outside the room, or staring down at a folder or document on the desk, while ignoring what you have to say.

Question

Which examples represent an individual not engaging in dialogue?

Options:

1. A salesman looks out the window and avoids giving direct answers

2. An engineer gives short, undemonstrative answers in reply to open-ended questions from his manager

3. A laboratory technician articulates her answers to address the questions put to her

4. A maintenance technician listens closely to what his supervisor is saying and responds when invited to

Answer:

Option 1: This option is correct. Being distracted and not answering questions directly is an example of a person not willing to engage in dialogue.

Option 2: This option is correct. Giving short answers to open-ended questions shows an unwillingness to engage in dialogue.

Option 3: This option is incorrect. Giving articulate responses to questions demonstrates a willingness to engage in dialogue.

Option 4: This option is incorrect. Listening closely and responding when asked demonstrates that the technician is willing to engage in dialogue.

The second challenge you may face during a difficult conversation occurs when the conversation takes a destructive direction. When this happens, the person you're talking with diverts the conversation from its original direction by claiming to be right, making accusations, or assigning blame. These directions are all equally damaging for conversations.

See each destructive direction that a conversation can go in to learn more about it.

Claiming to be right

Claiming to be right is when a person you are having a conversation with disturbs the direction of the discussion by making this claim about everything, while declaring that you and everyone else are wrong.

For example, the person may say, "Make no mistake: I'm completely right."

Making accusations

A conversation can go in a destructive direction when the person you're talking with starts to make accusations. People usually resort to making accusations when they feel threatened or vulnerable.

Here's an example. A person makes an accusation by saying, "You've singled me out on purpose!"

Assigning blame

When you're talking to a colleague about a performance-related problem, the person may assign blame to you or other colleagues for the problem.

Managing Difficult Conversations

For example, your colleague might respond to you by saying, "This has nothing to do with me. It's all your fault."

The third challenge you may face in a difficult conversation occurs when you're challenged by your own emotions. This may happen when you're criticized during the conversation. People normally have two automatic responses to criticism: respond angrily or respond defensively. These are also known as fight or flight reactions.

Both types of responses are defense mechanisms that are triggered in certain situations. You are likely to experience the urge to have a fight or flight reaction when you think the other person's behavior is wrong or you feel that you are being unfairly criticized.

The fight response represents a strong emotional reaction. You want to increase the level of confrontation. Your behavior can be perceived as being aggressive. This type of reaction can cause lasting damage to your working relationships with colleagues.

The flight response represents your desire to escape the situation or avoid confrontation. Your colleagues may have less respect for you if you choose this response. You also run the risk of being embarrassed.

Here's an example of a manager having a fight response during a conversation. Mike is the customer service manager of a software company. He is talking to Tom, a member of the customer service team, about a serious complaint a customer has made.

Tom accuses Mike of being unfamiliar with the product the customer complained about. Mike is upset and loses his temper.

He demands that Tom apologize to him or he'll face disciplinary action. Mike's response jeopardizes his working relationship with Tom.

In this example of a flight reaction, Rashaundra is a human resources manager with a construction company. She's having a conversation with Beth, the chief financial officer. Rashaundra is unhappy that Beth authorized the hiring of extra administrative staff without consulting her.

During the conversation, Beth justifies her decision by saying that the new employees were needed urgently and, if she had liaised with Rashaundra, the process would have taken too long.

Rashaundra is upset at the implication that she is too slow at her job. She becomes quiet and withdrawn. She abruptly ends the conversation and rushes from the room.

Question

Which examples represent challenges that you may face during a difficult conversation?

Options:

1. A supervisor is distracted and uncommunicative during a discussion with a senior manager

2. During a conversation to discuss a discipline issue, a hotel worker accuses her manager of targeting her

3. A manager at a hardware manufacturer reacts angrily to criticism during a conversation with a colleague

4. A manager at a recruitment company calmly pays attention when a junior consultant vents her frustration

5. A systems analyst asks her manager to outline the necessity for wanting to discuss her punctuality issues

6. A computer programmer blames his supervisor for causing the backlog of work

Answer:

Option 1: This option is correct. Not paying attention and being uncommunicative demonstrate that the person doesn't want to engage in dialogue.

Option 2: This option is correct. When the person being spoken to makes accusations, this is an example of the conversation taking a destructive direction.

Option 3: This option is correct. When a manager reacts angrily to criticism, he has been challenged by his own emotions. This is a fight response.

Option 4: This option is incorrect. Calmly paying attention while a colleague vents her frustration doesn't represent a challenge you may face during a difficult conversation. The conversation could have gone in a destructive direction if the colleague began to accuse the manager of targeting her.

Option 5: This option is incorrect. Asking a manager to outline the reasons for the conversation doesn't represent a challenge you may face during a difficult conversation. The conversation could have gone in a destructive direction if the analyst began to claim he was right.

Option 6: This option is correct. When a person assigns blame, this is an example of the conversation taking a destructive direction.

HANDLING DIFFICULT CONVERSATIONS

Handling difficult conversations

As a leader, you should be prepared to deal with the challenges that often come with difficult conversations. There are several strategies you can use to deal with these situations.

Question

How do you rate your ability to deal with challenges that can make a conversation difficult?

Options:

1. Excellent
2. Average
3. Poor

Answer:

Option 1: That's great. You've indicated that you rate your ability to deal with challenges that can make a conversation difficult as excellent. The rest of this course should give you even more tips.

Option 2: You've rated your ability to deal with challenges that can make a conversation difficult as

Managing Difficult Conversations

average. The rest of this course will provide you with valuable advice about how you might improve your ability.

Option 3: You've rated your ability to deal with challenges that can make a conversation difficult as poor. This is an area you have identified that you need to improve on. The rest of this course will provide you with valuable advice about how you might improve your ability.

Strategies to deal with challenges that you may face during difficult conversations are essential management tools. In the remainder of this topic, you'll learn about strategies for dealing with a person who doesn't engage in the conversation. In addition, you'll learn the strategies you can use to deal with a conversation that takes a destructive direction, and you'll learn what to do when you become challenged by your own emotions.

DEALING WITH NONENGAGEMENT

Dealing with nonengagement

When you deal with a person who won't engage with you, an effective strategy is to comment on the person's reaction and take control of the situation by asking questions. If the person is distracted by something else, make a comment about it. If the person ignores you completely, explain in a neutral tone how this makes you feel. You can use questions to probe the other person's point of view and to prompt justification from the person.

Anna is the manager of a graphic design company. She is having a conversation with Kelly, a graphic designer. Kelly has missed several deadlines for important clients. Anna is finding that Kelly doesn't want to engage with her. Follow along as Anna deals with this challenging situation.

Anna: Kelly, I want to hear your point of view so that we can reach a mutual understanding. You need to realize that meeting deadlines is crucial to keeping our clients happy.

Anna is supportive.

Managing Difficult Conversations

Kelly: OK.
Kelly is bored and indifferent.

Anna: It's good you agree with my point of view but I don't think you realize how serious missing deadlines can be for our company.
Anna is concerned.

Kelly: I'm not sure what you're trying to say...exactly.
Kelly is unsure.

Anna: Let me ask you this...what did you think of your last deadline? Was it too inflexible? Is there a reason you missed it that I should know about?
Anna is concerned.

Kelly: Well...actually...I kind of feel like I have designer's block. Ideas just don't come quick and easy like they used to. I don't know what to do.
Kelly is worried.

Anna: Kelly...listen. It's OK...it happens. Let's talk about some ideas and suggestions to get you back to your old self.
Anna is friendly.

Anna explained to Kelly how her reaction suggested that she didn't understand the importance of meeting her deadlines.

Then Anna asked Kelly some questions. Kelly finally decided to engage in the conversation and Anna was able to take control of the situation.

Question

Consider how Anna successfully dealt with Kelly. What would you do if the person you were talking with chose to ignore you completely?

Options:

1. Carry on making your point without commenting on the situation

2. Explain in a neutral tone how this makes you feel

3. Ask if the person is shy or not interested in having the conversation

Answer:

Option 1: This option is incorrect. Carrying on without commenting on the situation isn't going to help the conversation reach a successful outcome.

Option 2: This is the correct option. By explaining in a neutral tone how this makes you feel, you begin to engage the person by appealing to their emotions. Using a neutral tone prevents the person you are talking to from reacting defensively.

Option 3: This option is incorrect. Asking questions is only an effective strategy if the questions relate directly to the situation.

REFRAMING, VALIDATION, AND CRITICISM

Reframing, validation, and criticism

A conversation going in a destructive direction is the second difficult conversation challenge that you may face. The strategy for getting it back on track is to reframe unhelpful statements made by the person you're talking with. You can do this by changing unhelpful statements into helpful ones to facilitate creating progress during the conversation.

Being challenged by your own emotions is the third difficult conversation challenge. During difficult conversations, you may have strong emotions because you believe the other person's behavior or attitude is wrong. This is often what causes you to have a fight or flight reaction. To manage these emotions, you need to recognize that the other person's feelings are valid. You may not agree with them, but you should start by acknowledging them to keep the conversation open and productive.

It's also important to manage your response to criticism when you're challenged by your own emotions. If you find that you're about to react angrily or defensively to criticism during a conversation, you should identify what your emotions are. You should also avoid responding too soon to criticism.

Question

Match the strategy to the difficult conversation challenge it addresses. Each strategy may match to more than one challenge.

Options:

A. Comment on the person's reaction
B. Reframe unhelpful statements
C. Create validation
D. Manage your response to criticism
E. Take control by asking questions

Targets:

1. Person doesn't engage
2. Conversation takes a destructive direction
3. Challenged by your own emotions

Answer:

Commenting on the person's reaction and taking control by asking questions are examples of strategies used when a person doesn't engage.

Reframing unhelpful statements is an example of a strategy to use when a conversation takes a destructive direction.

Creating validation and managing your response to criticism are examples of strategies to use when you're challenged by your own emotions.

KEEPING CONVERSATIONS ON TRACK

Keeping conversations on track

One of the most challenging aspects of managing a difficult conversation is to keep the discussion on track. The person you're talking with may not like what you have to say and might try to make the conversation go in a different direction. Very often, that direction may be destructive in nature. Assigning blame, claiming to be right, and making accusations can cause a conversation to go in a destructive direction.

To get a conversation back on track, you reframe the discussion and move it toward a more constructive outcome. So, when the person you're talking with assigns blame, you should reframe what the person says by acknowledging contributions. When the person claims to be right, you reframe to establish both sides of the story. And when the person makes accusations, you reframe to outline impact and intention.

See each strategy for moving a conversation back to a constructive direction to learn more about it.

Acknowledge contributions

You acknowledge contributions by admitting that you may have also been partly responsible for the problem that has occurred.

For example, you could say, "Yes, maybe I did contribute to the problem. I think we both have. But let's move past that and try to find a solution."

Establish both sides of story

To establish both sides of the story, you ask for the other person's point of view. Then you share your current position with the person.

Here's an example of what you say to do this: "I want to be sure that I fully understand your perspective. You obviously feel strongly about this issue. But I'd also like to share my perspective with you."

Outline impact and intention

To outline impact and intention, you explain to the person that you realize how the situation, and your role in it, has affected the person. You then state that it wasn't your intention to make the person feel uneasy.

For example, you could say, "I can see that my decision has upset you. This wasn't my intention. The decision was made for the good of the company."

HOW TO REFRAME A CONVERSATION

How to reframe a conversation

You use the guidelines for reframing a conversation to achieve a successful outcome. By reframing, you help the person you are in conversation with make the transition from assigning blame, claiming to be right, or making accusations to a point where the person is an active contributor to the conversation.

Chris is a senior partner with an architecture firm. He's talking to Helen, a recent college graduate who has been working with the company for a year. Helen is unhappy that she hasn't been included in the team for a new project. She feels that she is being unfairly overlooked. Follow along as Chris uses the guidelines for reframing a conversation to achieve a successful outcome.

Helen: Here we go again...I don't get to work on the good project! I never get any opportunities!

Helen is frustrated.

Chris: I'm guessing you don't feel challenged? Is that it? You've completed a lot of projects for the company so far.

Chris is calm.

Helen: Since day one, I've been designing small-scale stuff. Renovations. But when the larger projects come along...nothing. What's the point of doing excellent work and delivering on time?

Helen is agitated.

Chris: It sounds like you feel undervalued and frustrated because you're not being challenged.

Chris is understanding.

Helen: Well, yeah! Everybody else gets the big projects, and I get the crumbs!

Helen is angry.

Chris: Ah, your colleagues. Think about it...they have more experience. And you may be fed up with small projects, but they're the bulk of the recent contracts. Those crumbs you're talking about are a key source of revenue. Your efforts are appreciated.

Chris is conciliatory.

Helen: OK, I get that I'm the least experienced architect here, but...

Helen is less agitated.

Chris: We know that you're a talented architect, and when the right thing comes along, you'll get your shot. You have to learn to walk before you can run.

Chris is supportive.

Helen: When you put it like that...I guess you have a point.

Helen is sheepish.

Chris listened to Helen. He extracted the core ideas of what she was saying. He identified that she felt unchallenged and mentioned this point to her on two occasions. He also developed relevant concepts in relation to the good work that Helen completed for the company as well as noting that she was the least experienced architect with the company. He persisted with these guidelines to move the conversation in a constructive direction.

REFRAMING TO ACHIEVE POSITIVE OUTCOMES

Reframing to achieve positive outcomes
Case Study
Scenario

Grace is an office manager. She is having a conversation with Sarah, an administrative assistant. Grace is concerned about Sarah's phone manner. Grace believes that Sarah isn't courteous enough and is too hasty when dealing with people on the phone. Follow along as Grace uses some of the guidelines for reframing a conversation to achieve a successful outcome.

Grace: I think you need to reconsider how you deal with people on the phone, Sarah. You're giving the impression that answering the phone is a burden. You're rushing to end calls.

Grace is concerned.

Sarah: Maybe the burden is my workload! Maybe if I wasn't overwhelmed by everything else, I could think about how I talk on the phone!

Sarah is defiant.

Grace: So you're saying your volume of work is making it difficult for you to perform at your best?
Grace is calm.
Sarah: You think? Maybe if you spent a bit more time in the office, you'd know the chaos we have to deal with every single day.
Sarah is resolute.
Grace: I hear you. Maybe I should be on hand a bit more. But for now, let's focus on how we can manage your workload better. You can't perform at your best if you have too many things to juggle at once.
Grace is calm.

Question

Which guidelines for framing a conversation to achieve a successful outcome did Grace use?

Options:
1. Extracted core ideas
2. Developed relevant concepts
3. Persisted
4. Exploited advantages
5. Was evasive

Answer:

Option 1: This option is correct. Grace mentioned that the volume of work was responsible for Sarah's poor performance.

Option 2: This option is correct. Grace developed the relevant concept of better managing workloads during her conversation with Sarah.

Option 3: This option is correct. Grace persisted in extracting core ideas from her conversation with Sarah. She mentioned twice how Sarah's workload was hindering her performance.

Option 4: This option is incorrect. Exploiting advantages isn't one of the guidelines for achieving a successful outcome.

Option 5: This option is incorrect. Being evasive isn't one of the guidelines for achieving a successful outcome.

CREATING VALIDATION

Creating validation

Sometimes, during a difficult conversation, your emotions may get the better of you. You might become frustrated and angry, or you might become upset and withdrawn. These emotions are part of your natural defenses. However, losing control of your emotions won't help you to achieve a successful outcome. In fact, these emotions lead to fight or flight behavior on your part. An angry response is an example of fight behavior, while a defensive response represents flight behavior.

A common trigger that can cause you to lose control of your emotions is when you sense that the other person's behavior is wrong. You may find what the person is saying to be objectionable, or that the person's behavior is dismissive and disrespectful. When you encounter a situation like this, you may experience fight or flight urges. This could mean you're tempted to address the issue angrily, or you could become upset and embarrassed and want to escape.

When you're in a difficult conversation that tests your emotional resolve, you may not want to acknowledge that the person's position or point of view is valid. But this is exactly what you need to do to manage the conversation.

This approach creates validation by normalizing the other person's feelings. Doing this neutralizes your own emotional response. This helps you to suppress your fight or flight reactions. It means that even if you are faced with difficult behavior in a conversation, you should take the higher road and not let your emotions control your reaction. Instead, you might have to concede that the other person's feelings or position are partly valid.

Making this allowance for the other person may make you feel uncomfortable. You might not like having to do it, but it's the best way to move the conversation back toward a successful path. It's important to note that this doesn't mean that you have to agree with the other person. By normalizing the other person's feelings, you're no longer likely to experience extreme fight or flight reactions. This will make you a much better communicator and increase your chances of achieving a successful outcome.

By normalizing the other person's feelings you can manage your own emotions, but you can also create a situation where the other person feels safe to speak. You normalize the person's feelings by validating the person's position. Validation can be carried out at three levels: acknowledgment, acceptance, and identification.

See each level of validation to learn more about it.

Acknowledgment

Acknowledgment is the entry level for creating validation. It's the easiest place to start when you want to normalize another person's feelings. Basically, you paraphrase what the person says. But you don't imply that you agree or disagree with what is being said.

Achieving acknowledgment is easier than achieving acceptance and identification because you're not introducing your own feelings to the conversation. So, even if you completely disagree with the person, by acknowledging what has been said, you're not committing yourself to making a judgment. Instead, you're just clarifying what the person said to prompt further discussion.

Acceptance

Acceptance is the next level of validation. It's a trickier level because you have to accept that the other person's feelings are valid. You may find this difficult to do, but acceptance has a strong emotional resonance that can contribute to a better dialogue. The person you're talking with may become more willing to engage once you have created validation through acceptance.

Identification

Identification is the third level of validation. It involves introducing your own personal experiences to the conversation. You convey to the person that you both share common experiences and feelings. But you still don't have to agree or disagree with the person.

Here are some examples of how each level of validation could be applied to a single scenario. In this instance, a manager has been given the uncomfortable task of informing a direct report that his hours are being cut back due to budgetary constraints. Naturally, he's angry about this. The manager could acknowledge his feelings by saying, "You're angry because this will affect your pay."

The manager could demonstrate acceptance by saying, "No one likes being asked to give up hours." And the manager could demonstrate identification by saying, "I've been asked to take a pay cut, too."

Question

Match the methods of creating validation to the statements that they represent. Not all statements will have a match.

Options:

A. Acknowledgment
B. Acceptance
C. Identification

Targets:

1. "I can tell that your colleague is irritating you."
2. "Nobody likes being told what to do."
3. "I often feel that I get no respect either."
4. "That's a ridiculous claim."

Answer:

Acknowledging that a person is irritated is a sign that you're validating that person's feelings. Acknowledgment is the first level for creating validation and involves paraphrasing what the person has said.

Saying that nobody likes being told what to do is an example of using acceptance to create validation. Acceptance is the second level of creating validation. At this level, you have to accept that the other person's feelings are valid.

This statement is an example of using identification to create validation. Identification is the third level of creating validation. This involves introducing your own personal experience to the conversation.

Managing Difficult Conversations

Saying that a claim is ridiculous is not a statement you could use to create validation. This statement would immediately cause the person you are talking with to become aggressive or defensive.

NORMALIZING A PERSON'S FEELINGS

Normalizing a person's feelings

Being able to normalize a person's feelings helps you to avoid losing control over your own emotions. Using the three levels for validating the person's position enables you to reassert your control over the conversation.

Case Study: Question 1 of 1
Scenario

For your convenience, the case study is repeated with each question.

Anna is a manager of a graphic design company. She previously spoke with Kelly, a graphic designer, about the quality of her recent work. Anna was unhappy with Kelly's level of engagement in that conversation. This time, Anna is trying to indicate that Kelly's feelings are valid, even though she doesn't really want to.

Kelly: You know what's really getting to me lately?
Kelly is aggrieved.
Anna: No, what?
Anna is careful.

Kelly: I'm not paid enough for the work I do around here.
Kelly is put out.
Anna: Well, no one likes being short of money.
Anna is concerned.
Kelly: That's for sure!
Kelly is agreeing.

Question:

Which level of validation did Anna use to normalize Kelly's feelings?

Options:

1. Acknowledgment
2. Acceptance
3. Identification

Answer:

Option 1: This option is incorrect. Anna didn't paraphrase what Kelly said. If she had acknowledged Kelly's feelings she might have said, "I can tell that you feel you're not being adequately rewarded."

Option 2: This is the correct option. Even though Anna might not have agreed with Kelly, she accepted that her feelings were valid. Anna didn't explicitly indicate that she agreed or disagreed with Kelly.

Option 3: This option is incorrect. Anna didn't introduce her own experience to the conversation. If Anna had identified with Kelly's feelings, she might have said, "You're not the only one, you know. We're all in the same boat."

NATURAL REACTIONS TO CRITICISM

Natural reactions to criticism

Being criticized is the second trigger that may cause you to experience strong emotions during a difficult conversation. This can also lead you to experience fight or flight reactions, which can jeopardize the conversation.

However, you can handle criticism in a difficult conversation by following a number of steps. First, you need to recognize your own reactions and then listen. Next, you should ask questions. And finally, you respond.

To complete the first step, recognizing your own reactions, you should identify the different features of your fight and flight reactions when you're experiencing them. When you're criticized, your natural defense mechanisms kick in and you feel like fighting the criticism, or running away from it.

There are tell-tale signs that you may be experiencing a fight response. You may feel angry, which can cause your pulse rate to spike. You may articulate your points using sharp jabbing gestures. You may make strong eye contact with the other person and talk in a louder tone. Your

Managing Difficult Conversations

overall demeanor may become more animated causing you to speak over the other person.

When criticism provokes your flight response, you may find yourself avoiding direct eye contact with the person. In addition, your demeanor becomes submissive – your head is likely down and your shoulders are hunched. You may start to fidget nervously and speak in a quiet tone and begin to stutter.

Question

Which examples demonstrate fight or flight responses during a difficult conversation?

Options:

1. A supervisor with a catering company points her finger sharply during a conversation with a colleague

2. A sales manager raises his voice during a meeting with a member of the sales team

3. A car assembly line manager becomes flushed during a conversation with a fellow manager

4. A production engineer begins to stutter nervously during a conversation with another engineer

5. A production coordinator remains calm during a conversation with a supplier

6. A project manager listens closely to what her colleague is saying

Answer:

Option 1: This option is correct. Using jabbing gestures such as pointing a finger is an example of a fight response. The person you are talking with may find this gesture to be insulting or even threatening.

Option 2: This option is correct. Raising your voice during a meeting is a feature of a fight response. If you raise your voice it means that you've lost your cool and let your aggressive emotions take control.

Option 3: This option is correct. Becoming flushed during a conversation is an indicator of a flight response. It's a visible sign that you're uncomfortable with the situation and you want it to end as soon as possible.

Option 4: This option is correct. Stuttering is an example of a flight response. Perhaps a situation has made you feel nervous and uneasy. When this happens, you may become flustered and stutter as a result.

Option 5: This option is incorrect. Remaining calm isn't a feature of a fight or flight response.

Option 6: This option is incorrect. Listening closely isn't an example of a fight or flight response.

The second step to handle criticism in a difficult conversation is to listen. Instead of becoming clouded by your emotions, you should listen so that you can clearly understand the other person's issue.

Listening also allows you to demonstrate that you respect the other person's perspective. By listening, you show that you're willing to let the person speak without interruption.

Crucially, listening also gives you the opportunity to compose yourself. Listening buys you time to identify your fight or flight response and take control of your emotions.

TAKING STEPS TO HANDLE CRITICISM

Taking steps to handle criticism

The third step to handle criticism during a difficult conversation is to ask questions. Use your questions to find out more details about the issue and how it began. You might be able to discover if the issue is a one time thing, or if it has been developing over a long period. You can also ask questions to keep the other person occupied and to buy time so that you can compose yourself.

When you ask questions during a difficult conversation, it's very important that you use a neutral tone of voice. By using a neutral tone of voice, you send a message that you want to discuss the issue rationally.

If you sound overly aggressive or defensive, the other person will respond accordingly. An aggressive tone may cause the person to disengage from the conversation or try to match your level of aggression. The person may also try to capitalize on your aggression by using it as an excuse to try and get away from the situation. In either case, this could result in a difficult conversation.

The final step for handling criticism during a difficult conversation is to respond. Once you've completed the other steps by recognizing your own reactions, listening, and asking questions, you're then in a strong position to respond. There are three options you can use to respond. You can agree, disagree, or ask for more time.

See each response option to learn more about it.

Agree

No one likes accepting criticism, but it's a part of life. You might have to concede that the person's criticism of you is valid. On the plus side, the conversation will end with the other person respecting you for your maturity and honesty. And you can learn from the person's feedback so that you can prevent the issue from occurring again.

For example, a software designer agrees with a colleague by saying, "I hear what you're saying, and you're right. I won't do that again."

Disagree

You can respond to the criticism by disagreeing. However, the conversation should remain constructive as you outline your reasons.

For instance, a chief financial officer disagrees with a payroll manager by saying, "I can see how the situation looks from your perspective. But I don't see things in the same way." If the chief financial officer had responded emotionally in a fight or flight manner, the conversation would likely end badly.

Ask for more time

You use this option if you've been surprised by the person's criticism. Or you can use it if you still feel that your emotions are getting the better of you even after completing the previous three steps.

For example, a procurement manager asks for more time after being surprised by criticism from a colleague. "This has come as a bit of a shock. I'm going to need some time to think about what you've said."

HANDLING CRITICISM EFFECTIVELY

Handling criticism effectively

Returning to Anna – the manager of a graphic design company – and her conversation with Kelly, a graphic designer. The conversation becomes difficult for Anna when Kelly criticizes her. Follow along to see how Anna handles this criticism.

Kelly: It's no surprise I've been struggling lately. Any time I come to you for advice, you're either too busy or not here.

Kelly is accusatory.

Anna: OK...Tell me more.

Anna is neutral.

Kelly: That's all I've got to say about it.

Kelly is direct and matter-of-fact.

Anna: You're finding work difficult at the moment. Understood! But did you really make a proper effort to bring this to my attention?

Anna is neutral.

Kelly: Actually, I did.

Kelly is stubborn.

Anna: I know things aren't easy for you at the moment. However, I disagree with your criticism. I always ensure that I'm available for my team.
Anna is neutral.

Anna used the four steps for handling criticism to remain in control of her emotions. After first hearing Kelly's criticism of her, Anna experienced an aggressive fight response. But she invited Kelly to say more so she could listen and take the time to compose herself. Then she put a question to Kelly in a very neutral tone. Finally, she responded to Kelly by disagreeing with her, using a neutral tone.

IDENTIFYING STEPS TO HANDLE CRITICISM

Identifying steps to handle criticism
Question
Which examples demonstrate the steps you should take to handle criticism during a difficult conversation?
Options:
1. A sales manager realizes she is experiencing a flight response because she is fidgeting nervously, so she begins to control her emotions
2. A manufacturing supervisor composes himself while listening to what his colleague has to say
3. Using a neutral tone of voice, a call center team leader asks a team member a question to find out more about the issue
4. A human resources manager agrees with her colleague's criticism of her
5. An owner of an engineering company uses an aggressive tone to question an employee
6. A publicity manager becomes flushed and asks to end the meeting

Managing Difficult Conversations

Answer:

Option 1: This option is correct. Recognizing the features of your emotional reaction during a meeting is the first step for handling criticism in a difficult conversation.

Option 2: This option is correct. Listening to what the other person has to say is the second step for dealing with criticism. In addition to buying time to allow you to compose yourself, listening enables you to gain a better understanding of the issue and to show respect for the other person.

Option 3: This option is correct. Asking questions is the third step for handling criticism. As well as allowing you to find out more about the issue, questioning gives you time to control your response and convey to the other person that you are willing to have a mature and constructive discussion.

Option 4: This option is correct. Responding is the final step for handling criticism. You can respond in three ways, by agreeing, disagreeing, or asking for more time.

Option 5: This option is incorrect. Using an aggressive tone to ask a question may cause the other person to disengage from the conversation.

Option 6: This option is incorrect. The manager should have identified that he was experiencing a flight response and managed his emotions, rather than asking to end the meeting.

REFERENCES

References

The Tackling Difficult Conversations Pocketbook - 2009, Peter English, Management Pocketbook

Difficult Conversations: How to Discuss What Matters Most - 2000, Douglas Stone, Bruce Patton, Sheila Heen, Penguin

Find Your Courage: 12 Acts for Becoming Fearless at Work and in Life - 2009, Margie Warrell, McGraw-Hill

Failure to Communicate: How Conversations Go Wrong and What You Can Do to Right Them - 2010, Holly Weeks, Harvard Business Press

Speaking Your Mind in 101 Difficult Situations - 2002, Don Gabor, Conversation Arts Media

How to Tell Anyone Anything: Breakthrough Techniques for Handling Difficult Conversations at Work - 2009, Richard S. Gallagher

The Tackling Difficult Conversations Pocketbook - 2009, Peter English, Management Pocketbooks

GLOSSARY

Glossary
A
activity - A task or set of tasks in action.
authority - The power or right to give orders and instructions and to make decisions.
B
bias - A personal opinion, preference, or inclination toward something that is formed without objective justification.
blaming - Making statements that attribute fault or accountability for a negative outcome to some other person or situation.
body language - Non-verbal communication consisting of posture, gestures, body position, facial expressions, and eye contact. Often culturally specific in meaning.
brainstorming - The act of generating ideas, often performed in team settings.

business culture - A system of shared assumptions, beliefs, and values that influence the behavior of people operating within an organizational structure.

business etiquette - Formal and informal etiquette and rules of order applying to interactions with coworkers, work colleagues, and business partners within a business, industry, or economy. See etiquette.

C

company - An organization that is a legal entity operating for profit. See organization.

complaint - An expression of feelings of pain, dissatisfaction, or resentment, often directed toward a specific person, object, or situation.

context - The social circumstances or environments that determine, refine, or change the implicit meaning of a communicated message.

corporate culture - See business culture.

coworker - A person working with another worker, usually at or near a similar level of authority or responsibility in the workplace hierarchy.

D

disinterest - Objectivity uninfluenced by bias or prejudice.

dynamics - The interplay of different forces on any particular activity.

E

eloquence - The expression of emotional content in a formal communication method using persuasive and inspiring language.

empathy - The ability to feel and understand the concerns of others.

empowerment - Giving a person the authority to make decisions without requiring specific approval. See authority.

engagement - Emotional and psychological commitment to completing tasks and attaining organizational goals and objectives.

environment - The political, strategic, or operational context within, or external to, the organization.

etiquette - A set of written and unwritten rules of conduct that govern social interactions within a culture, social class, or group.

F

false assumption - A conclusion that is not based in fact, or is based on incomplete knowledge of the facts.

faux pas - An unintentional violation of accepted social norms, such as customs or etiquette.

feedback - Information communicated to an individual, work unit, or team about job-related performance or behavior.

G

goals - Quantifiable aims used to measure progress toward an end result.

I

influence - The power to change an outcome by affecting or controlling a course of events.

initiative - An organizational program, project, or effort that has a specific purpose, goals, and objectives. See project.

M

micromanagement - A leadership style in which a manager or other leader monitors the activities of a person or group very closely, often to the detriment of the organization.

motivation - Energy directed toward completing tasks and achieving goals and objectives.

mutual agreement - An obvious or implied agreement between employees or between an employee and an employer.

N

need - A requirement to achieve a goal or objective.

nonverbal communication - Unspoken or unvoiced elements of communication used to send messages, modify meaning, and convey emotion. See also body language.

O

objective - A specific measurable or observable goal to be achieved over a specified period of time.

organization - A defined group of people who have common goals and who follow an agreed upon set of operating procedures to produce products and services.

organizational structure - See structure.

P

performance - The degree to which objectives have been accomplished relative to preset

personal bias - See bias.

persuasion - A form of communication that uses logical arguments and evidence to gain support.

plan - A detailed formulation of a program of action for achieving a goal or objective.

polite fiction - A situation where participants are aware of a truth, but pretend to believe in an alternative version of events to avoid conflict or embarrassment.

positive reinforcement - Specific praise or rewards targeted at a subject with the purpose of increasing the future frequency of a desired behavior.

prejudice - Negative attitudes toward or preconceived judgments of individuals or groups.

progress - Movement toward achieving stated objectives.

project - A collaborative enterprise with a defined beginning and end that is planned to achieve particular goals and objectives.

R

rank - A person's position within a defined hierarchy.

rapport - Harmonious accord between two people or one person and an audience.

resistance - Noncompliant behavior.

S

skill - The capability to perform a specific task or achieve a specific goal or objective.

status - A person's social or cultural value or standing relative to that of others.

structure - The design of the delegation of authority, division of labor, and areas of control within an organization.

T

thought pattern - A logical progression of reasoning.

transparency - Actions and communication free from pretense or deceit.

U

undermine - Intentionally creating obstacles to another individual's pursuit of success.

V

values - Shared beliefs that are the basis for ethical action within a business culture. See business culture.

W

work environment - A person's position within a defined hierarchy.

www.ingramcontent.com/pod-product-compliance
Lightning Source LLC
Chambersburg PA
CBHW020914180526
45163CB00007B/2736